HERITAGE TREES OF IRELAND

To Mary Keenan,
who nursed this tree project
from conception to delivery:
this is her seedling.

HERITAGE TREES OF IRELAND

FOREWORD BY THOMAS PAKENHAM

AUBREY FENNELL

PHOTOGRAPHY BY CARSTEN KRIEGER & KEVIN HUTCHINSON

The Collins Press

First published in 2013 by
The Collins Press
West Link Park
Doughcloyne
Wilton
Cork

A CIP record for this book is available from the British Library.

ISBN: 978-1-84889-159-3

Design and typesetting by Fairways Design
Typeset in Palatino
Printed in Poland by Białostockie Zakłady Graficzne SA

Tree Council
of Ireland

Society of Irish Foresters

The Tree Council of Ireland wishes to acknowledge the generous support of the board and management of the Kerry Group in the publication of this book.

A few minutes ago every tree was excited, bowing to the roaring storm, waving, swirling, tossing their branches in glorious enthusiasm like worship. But though to the outer ear these trees are now silent, their songs never cease.

John Muir, Environmentalist

CONTENTS

Other Natives

The Europeans

Sacred Trees 161

Landmark & Junction Trees 179

Great Avenues & Historic Landscapes 199

Trees from the Orient   311

Foreword by Thomas Pakenham

Most of us like trees, and some are their passionate admirers. And yet we take them for granted. The oldest? The tallest? The fattest? Perhaps these superlatives grip our imagination. But how far beyond can we go? Our knowledge of the history of individual trees is astonishingly poor. An oak 500 years old has lived through 20 human generations – a witness to famines, wars, revolutions. And yet no one appears to know who planted it or why or when. It is almost as if this vast creature, rising to the height of a ten-storey building, has been invisible in the midst of us, lost in a mysterious fog.

In this inspiring book, Aubrey Fennell has done his best to dispel some of that fog. He is perfect for the romantic role of tree hunter. A daredevil tree surgeon by background (he once fell 60 feet out of a tree before his safety rope snatched him up a few feet from the ground), he joined us at the Irish Tree Society soon after its foundation in 1990. We created the Society to focus attention on important specimen trees. Many trees, we knew, were at risk from damage or destruction – less from ill will than from simple ignorance. But to protect them we needed to know where they were. Aubrey took up the vital task of hunting them down and listing them. Until then there had been no systematic listing of Irish trees, although a number of tree enthusiasts, including the late Alan Mitchell, had begun the mighty task. (In fact, Alan had generously helped me launch the Tree Society. It was he who that same afternoon led the first foray across the barbed wire to see the surviving trees in the half-abandoned arboretum at Headfort, County Meath.)

With a helping hand from both the Tree Council of Ireland and the National Botanic Gardens at Glasnevin, to add to the support of the Tree Society,

Aubrey then began a 15-year quest to hunt down and record important trees. Trees had always fascinated him. Now they became his obsession. I daren't think how many thousands of miles he travelled by car and on foot, tramping the bogs and glens in search of giants and other wonders. And now you can see the results of his Arthurian quest. (An oak over 30 feet in girth is described by Aubrey as the 'Holy Grail'.)

The trees described in this book are Aubrey's personal selection. Many, like the King Oak at Charleville near Tullamore, have been well known and admired for many years, however obscure their early history. Others will be a revelation to most people. Which one of us had ever heard of the Hanging Oak of Shane's Castle or the Grasping Birch of Sandyford or the Demented Beech at Parkanaur? My own favourite is, somewhat inevitably, the Squire's Walking Stick in the demesne at Tullynally, my home in Westmeath. This is an oak that was first described in print in 1838 when J. C. Loudon, the world's leading tree expert of that time, drew attention to the extraordinary straightness of the trunk. The tree was then a stripling, he reported, about 96 years old. Now it's a handsome middle-aged fellow of about 270 with what Aubrey calls 'the finest clean straight trunk in the country.' I hope it keeps its good looks for the next 300 years.

Thomas Pakenham
Chairman, the Irish Tree Society

Foreword by The Kerry Group

The Kerry Group is delighted to be associated with this excellent publication which catalogues Ireland's most important heritage trees. Most of these trees are located on farmland throughout the country and include champion trees, holy wells and fairy forts which have been maintained by our farming community down through the millennia. However, with the excellent photography of Carsten Krieger and Kevin Hutchinson, along with the associated stories articulated by Aubrey Fennell in this book, these trees are brought to life and given a new meaning for a wider audience.

It is appropriate that we focus on this remnant of our heritage because trees play, and have traditionally played, such an important part in our lives. We at Kerry are acutely aware of the universal impact of climate change and the need to stimulate economic and business development in a sustainable manner. We are actively addressing the challenges posed by climate change and have programmes in place to measure, manage and reduce climate change impacts. One way we can improve our environment is by planting more trees but also by managing and appreciating the trees we already have.

Partnership is essential to addressing solutions for complex environmental challenges and it is with this in mind that we are delighted to support this initiative. Kerry Group works with governments, non-governmental organisations and customers to understand the environmental issues we face. In this regard, Kerry has a proud record of supporting community initiatives and charitable causes. Right through its history, from its origins in the co-oper-

ative sector in Ireland, the Group has committed significant financial resources and considerable management and employee time in assisting with development of facilities, amenities and charitable projects in the communities within which it operates. This philosophy continues to be a core value of the Kerry organisation and, on an annual basis, the Group sponsors a wide range of education, health-care, sporting, leisure, arts, amenity, community development and charitable causes. Kerry continues to play a vital role in supporting local communities and in participating in community development programmes throughout the world.

We hope that this publication will help to preserve our heritage trees and will result in trees being appreciated by a wider audience. We are aware that the rural communities have an affinity with the natural environment while many urban dwellers have a more limited opportunity to interact with that environment. We hope that the publication of this book will be a building block to linking more and more people towards an appreciation of our natural environment and towards generating acknowledge-ment and respect for the vital part of our history and heritage that are our trees.

Stan Mc Carthy, CEO
The Kerry Group

Measuring Trees

A Personal Journey

I had the good fortune to grow up surrounded by trees in the corner of an old estate in County Carlow. We had a farm guesthouse and even visiting foresters could not identify some of our trees. A visit to Mount Usher Gardens in County Wicklow in my teens helped answer some of those questions and awaken my lifelong interest in naming and planting unusual trees. After finishing my education, I became a tree surgeon but that career came to a shattering halt when I dropped a tree onto an expensive parked car in Ballsbridge, Dublin. It was the impetus needed to work abroad and backpack around the world. Returning permanently to Ireland in 1997, I soon became aware of the Irish Tree Society as an organisation which shared my passion. Inspired by Thomas Pakenham, its founder, and encouraged by many new friends in the Society, I began to record and measure exceptional trees locally. Soon County Carlow was not big enough and I slipped into neighbouring counties. With increasing boldness, I went nationwide and knocked on many doors with what must have seemed an odd request.

Trees were first recorded in Ireland by Samuel Hayes in the 1790s, followed by J. C. Loudon in the 1820s who corresponded with many of the large estates. In the early 20th century, Elwes and Henry published the epic Trees of Great Britain and Ireland which includes many photographs and measurements of Irish trees. H. M. FitzPatrick updated many of these records for the 1932 International Conifer Conference. In the 1960s, the Tree Register of the British Isles was founded by Alan Mitchell, one of most renowned tree experts in the world. Assisted by Tony Hanan of John F. Kennedy Arboretum, together they recorded some 3,000 trees in about 70 estates in Ireland. The rest of the country was a blank space. What an opportunity to find new champions! Looking for trees is never dull and involves research and detective work but the advantage is that they do not move, unlike other hunter-gathering pursuits such as birdwatching. The tools needed are a hypsometer for measuring height, tape measure for girth, camera for its portrait and pocket guide for identification. Also useful are the old half-inch Ordnance Survey maps showing demesnes, and binoculars for scouting the landscape for tall silver firs and sequoias which regularly signpost tree collections. Unfortunately, nearly all of our woodlands had disappeared by 1700 and we now have very few trees over 500 years old. What we see now are 18th- and 19th-century plantings behind the walls of the Anglo-Irish estates, many of which were grant aided by the then British Government via the Dublin Society (now the Royal Dublin Society). We have an abundance of hedgerows with massive old ash, oak, beech and sycamore which are under constant threat from modern farming practices. Smaller species such as wild cherry, crab apple, aspen and hawthorn reveal themselves when in flower or autumn colour while everywhere are exotic species which thrive in our gentle climate.

In 2000, the planets aligned for me when I was invited to become recorder for the newly established Tree Register of Ireland. What joy! The Tree Register was initiated by the Tree Council of Ireland with funding from the Forest Service and the Irish Tree Society. Over 5,000 trees were recorded in the initial survey and another 5,000 added to the database in the intervening years. It became apparent as time went by that many important heritage trees did not meet the criteria of size, age or rarity to justify inclusion in a database of champion trees. Therefore, a heritage tree survey was begun in 2009, jointly funded by the Tree Council of Ireland, the Heritage Council, the Irish Tree Society and Crann. With the assistance of Kate Crane, we recorded 1,200 trees over the next two years, most of which can now be viewed on the Tree Council of Ireland's website: www.treecouncil.ie.

It is my hope that my tree measuring has been useful to show us what trees grow well and where and that individual trees are appreciated and given better protection. We need to safeguard these trees and pass them on to the next generation. They provide, after all, the very air that we breathe.

Aubrey Fennell
2013

How Old is a Tree?

Unless one knows the planting date of a tree, the only certain way that the age can be determined is by counting the annual growth rings. Short of cutting the tree down, this can only be done by using an auger and a core sample taken for analysis which is not recommended as it can be injurious to the health of the tree. The older the tree, the more likely it is to be hollow, making it impossible to date. By studying the growth rate of trees with a known planting date, we can estimate the likely age of a tree by measuring its girth at the standard 1.5m above the ground. Different species grow at different rates. Yews grow very slowly and live a long time while a poplar grows very fast and would be extremely old at 150 years. An oak growing in a forest would take twice as long to reach 6m in girth than one in an open field with a broad crown unhampered by neighbouring trees. Factors such as climate, soil and location will also have an effect and, like people, trees will grow into different shapes and sizes. I found the late Alan Mitchell's rule of an increase in girth of 1 inch/2.5cm a year for the more common species such as oak, beech, lime or ash to be the most useful and a tree of 10ft/3m in girth is probably about 120 years old. Below is an age estimate for various species.

Yew	
Girth =	Age (Years)
2m	150
3m	250
4m	350
5m	500
6m	700

Oak, Ash or Lime	
Girth =	Age (Years)
3m	120
4m	150
5m	200
6m	250
7m	320

Poplar, Sequoia or Monterey Cypress	
Girth =	Age (Years)
3m	40
4m	60
5m	80
6m	100
7m	120

THE
GREAT
OAKS

Oaks are the aristocrats of Ireland's tree world, and there
was a time when a mythical squirrel could travel from one end
of the country to the other without leaving the oak canopy. Sadly
oak woods were so decimated by medieval times that woodpeckers, dependent on the oaks for survival, became extinct. But
suddenly in recent years woodpeckers have returned to breed again,
and have become a wonderful symbol of renewal and regeneration as
the planting of broadleaf trees expands.

The sessile oak was designated Ireland's National Tree in 1990, but
in fact throughout history it has always been subservient to the ash in
Irish tradition. Ash is more widespread throughout the country, and
it grows taller. What is undeniable is that oak trees are among the
oldest, tallest, fattest and heaviest of all living things in Ireland.
Each tree should be cherished and protected as a living monument.

It is the most important woodland tree as it provides a
habitat for more species of wildlife than any other tree. The
widespread planting of oaks on estates in the 18th and
19th centuries has left us with a legacy of many large
mature trees in the prime of their potentially
long lives, and the following pages feature
a wide variety of prize specimens.

The King Oak

Charleville Estate, Tullamore, County Offaly
Quercus robur | **Pedunculate Oak**

HEIGHT:	19m
GIRTH:	8.29m
ACCESS:	The tree is located on private property but can be viewed on the driveway from the entrance gate.

The mightiest oak on the edge of the mightiest oakwood in Ireland can be seen at Charleville Forest near Tullamore. This common oak forest is a remnant of what the Irish landscape must have looked like before the destruction and loss of our forests in medieval times. The status of common oak as an Irish native tree has often been debated by ecologists. Most of the oaks we see now were originally planted by landowners in the 18th and 19th centuries. But core-dating of the oaks at Charleville show them to be between 350 and 450 years old, a lot older than any known introduction.

Common or pedunculate oak woods are generally found on base-rich soils such as the limestone of the midlands. They often incorporate a mixture of ash, elm and downy birch above an understorey of hazel, hawthorn and spindle. There are many large barrel-chested oaks scattered through the adjoining parkland. Some are even bigger in girth than the King Oak but fall short of its majestic presence.

The King Oak grows near the Tullamore entrance to the Charleville estate. It is an amazing tree as four of its lower branches stretch out, dipping and rising and dipping again over the ground up to 27m away. It defies the laws of gravity. There is a tradition that should any of its branches snap off, a member of the Hutton-Bury family will die. They own the estate so they have taken the understandable precaution of supporting the branches with wooden props. They should have thought of a lightning conductor, because in 1963 a thunderbolt struck, creating a gash down the trunk to the ground. The head of the family died soon afterwards. Today the tree is a popular meeting point for young and old. This is a privately owned estate but visitors are welcome providing they treat the woods with respect. This is one Royal that any Irishman would have no problem bowing to.

The King Oak
at Charleville Estate

Oldest Oak in Ireland

Abbey Leix Estate, Abbeyleix, County Laois
Quercus robur | **Pedunculate Oak**

HEIGHT: 17m
GIRTH: 7.03m
ACCESS: The tree is located on private property and is not open for public access.

Abbey Leix Estate is home to one of only two large pedunculate oak woodlands in Ireland, the other being Charleville in County Offaly. The Abbey Leix woods extend over some 120 hectares beside the River Nore on deep alluvial soils which flood in winter when they take on the appearance of the Louisiana swamps. It has been managed over time with selective removal of timber, but it still retains the character of primeval forest. One section called Parkhill is magical in May when it becomes a sea of bluebells as far as the eye can see. Jenkinstown Wood in County Kilkenny has the same effect and is accessible to the public.

Abbey Leix Estate is private and is only open occasionally to interested groups. It was home to the de Vesci family for 300 years before being sold in 1995. Since then the house and grounds have undergone extensive restoration with the parkland, gardens and lake renewed, attention to woodland management and new tree collections added.

One oak tree in particular has long been revered by the de Vesci family as 'The Old Oak', and is reputed to be the same tree mentioned by the diarist John Evelyn in the late 17th century as being then one of the oldest in Ireland. Found in a corner of the woods near the river, its protective Victorian cage has been removed in recent years. The oak is next mentioned by Samuel Hayes, who compiled the first book on trees in Ireland in 1794, when he wrote: '… but the finest trees by far are at Abbeyleix, we may here find an Oak of 20 feet 6 inches in circumference or nearly 7 feet diameter at a foot from the ground.'

Today it is 23 feet or 7m in girth at breast height, with a large gaping cavity where its leaning trunk lost a huge branch back in the mists of antiquity. It supports a large amount of epiphytic ferns, moss and lichen and the crown looks good, considering its great age. So how old could this tree be? It certainly looks to be the same tree that claimed to be 'The Old Oak' down the years, not another that has inherited its crown, as often happens at holy wells when the original dies. If we can rely on our sources then it must be between 500 to 700 years old which makes it a living monumental treasure. Putting it in context I quote Dr Oliver Rackham, the world-renowned authority on trees and woodland, '10,000 oaks of 100 years are no substitute for one 500-year-old oak tree'.

Cave-like and hollow inside – Ireland's Oldest Oak Tree at Abbey Leix Estate

Harley Park Oak

Harley Park, Ballingarry, County Tipperary
Quercus robur | **Pedunculate Oak**

HEIGHT: 13m
GIRTH: 8.17m
ACCESS: The tree is located on private property. Viewing is by prior appointment only.

South Kilkenny and Tipperary is a world unto itself of gentle hills and river valleys. Waves of immigrants from the Normans to the Anglo-Irish put down very deep roots, and the landscape has a look of continuity and richness found nowhere else in Ireland. It is a place I visit time and time again to look for the tree hunter's Holy Grail which is an oak of 9m/30ft girth or more.

The tree that really started my obsession may be found just inside County Tipperary on the road between Callan and Ballingarry. At the gate-lodge entrance to Harley Park there is enough parking space for two cars. Beware of speeding traffic coming around a blind corner. The other side of the road has a stile into a large pasture field. In the middle of the field is the pot-bellied pig of Irish oak trees. When I first put my tape measure around the tree at the standard 1.5m above the ground it measured 9.8m. I had reached nirvana but then the tape slipped under its paunch and tightened up to 8.2m. I knew I could not claim it as a new Irish champion and the search had to go on for that elusive 30-footer. But what a great tree! Its short, squat trunk supports a small crown of branches pollarded about a hundred years ago. It is probably not that ancient, as its girth is exaggerated by a massive burr. Indentations on the bark suggest parts of the human anatomy.

Burrs are a result of irregular masses of buds that come to nothing but persist to form burrs. Timber grows around the burrs, and its grain goes all over the place, such as in this extreme case. The wood, with its intricate grain and colour, is highly prized for veneer and woodturning.

With its appearance of pregnancy maybe it should be called the 'Mother Oak'. In the Age of Discovery, whole continents were called after people. Why not trees?

The pot-bellied oak at Harley Park

Mountshannon Oak

Oak House, Mountshannon, County Clare
Quercus robur | **Common or Pedunculate Oak**

Height: 32m
Girth: 9.15m
Access: The tree is located on private property but can be viewed from the front gates to the property.

At the turn of the 20th century Augustine Henry, a native of Northern Ireland and one of the world's greatest plant collectors and discoverer of new species, commented that 'Ireland, renowned in ancient days for its oak timber, which was valued abroad, is now singularly wanting in even good specimens of solitary oak trees'. Maybe he was right. Compared to Britain, which has more ancient trees than any other nation in Europe, Ireland had very few big oaks. At that time Ireland was at its lowest ebb, with less than one per cent tree cover, the lowest in Europe. It was also a time when the estates of the Ascendancy, which might have harboured great trees, were being divided up in the greatest transfer of ownership in 200 years. The destruction of mature timber continued for another 50 years. Recent timber production has raised forest cover to ten per cent, so would Henry's comments still hold good today? My subjective criteria as to what makes a good specimen oak is a single stem of at least 6m girth, and I have found over 200 trees exceeding that, with over 40 exceeding 7.5m. Historically the fattest oak recorded was a long-gone tree of 8.5m girth recorded in Belvoir Park near Belfast in the 19th century. In 2000 two trees were co-champions at 8.8m. Finding a 9.1m/30-foot oak would give a tree hunter the most fun while keeping his clothes on, but it proved elusive. That is, until I returned to one of those champions at Oak House, Mountshannon, beside the River Shannon in 2009.

Oak House was the stable premises to the now derelict Mountshannon House. Behind the house the ground drops dramatically so that the tree's trunk is hidden to all but the livestock grazing beyond. What is unmissable is the huge crown over 30m high that overshadows the house and terrace. This is not an ancient tree that has had time to reach its monumental size, and it may be no older than the founding of Mountshannon village in 1742. Being struck by lightning has not slowed its growth, and when the tape stretched around the trunk I had reached the tree hunter's nirvana and the first oak in Ireland of 9.1m/30 feet girth.

Carsten Krieger at
the Mountshannon Oak

Estuary Oak at Tarbert

Tarbert, County Kerry
Quercus robur | **Pedunculate Oak**

HEIGHT: 6m
GIRTH: 2.36m
ACCESS: Public

On the lower reaches of the Shannon estuary, where County Limerick meets Kerry, lies the village of Tarbert. A coastal road links the village with Tarbert Island where a ferry crosses the Shannon Estuary to Killimer in County Clare, thus avoiding the 129km detour to cross the Shannon at Limerick city. Along the 3km stretch between village and pier lies the old Leslie estate of Tarbert House which dates from the 17th century, and still retains many fine oak trees and woods from the 18th century.

Opposite the main entrance to the house stands a remarkable stunted oak tree growing out of the stone embankment that keeps the road safely above the tidal estuary. A specially constructed retaining wall bulges out over the river and prevents the oak from sliding into the estuary. Without historical evidence it is difficult to say whether the tree was planted as a curious feature, or whether elaborate steps were taken to protect an existing tree during the construction of the road embankment. How it came to be here is of little consequence to the oak, as it has seized its chance and is doing just fine, with its roots curling above the saline water under the road. The oak is small at 6m high and 2.36m girth, and may be 150 years old. It certainly lives up to its Latin name of *'robur'* meaning strength, power or heart. It has needed all these qualities to endure the constant buffeting that the wind throws at it. You have to respect this born survivor.

Squire's Walking Stick

Tullynally Castle, Castlepollard, County Westmeath
Quercus robur | **Common or Pedunculate Oak**

HEIGHT: 34m
GIRTH: 4.68m
ACCESS: This tree is located in private property but may be viewed from the estate road to Tullynally.

Thomas Pakenham has done more than anyone to inspire people to appreciate the silent giants of the natural world through his books on remarkable trees on these islands and worldwide. It was meeting him and joining the Irish Tree Society which set me on my own voyage to hunt down Ireland's great trees.

Visiting Tullynally is a must for all tree lovers, and walking up to the Squire's Walking Stick is to pay homage at its shrine. It was planted in about 1745 in the park by the main avenue, and it now towers to its height of 34m on what is the finest clean straight oak trunk in the country. It has a deceptive girth of 4.7m without any apparent taper to the first branch at 12.1m. The stupendous form cannot be explained by genetics alone, but it must have had long-gone competition to help draw it up. A tree, if given space as in this parkland setting, will maximise its leaf coverage to utilise the sun's energy by spreading far and wide. During the 18th century, landowners were encouraged to plant oaks as a patriotic duty, as there was a shortage of timber for the Royal Navy to build the ships on which the Empire depended. Tall straight oaks, like the Squire's Walking Stick, provided the keel and planking while broad angular branches were used for the brackets that held the ships together. Luckily for us this tree escaped the saw, as steam and iron replaced wind and timber. But the demise of wooden ships was a bad thing overall, as falling demand led to a decline in planting.

Nearby are many magnificent tall stout beeches, while a silver fir by the edge of the park is the finest specimen in Ireland. Thomas Pakenham has developed an arboretum near the walled garden, and every year brings further expansion into the woods as he plants saplings grown from seeds acquired on his expeditions to the Far East. If you are lucky enough to have a guided tour from the man himself, you are in for a memorable treat.

The Squire's Walking Stick at Tullynally Castle owned by Thomas Pakenham – an oak tree with a uniquely straight and tall trunk

Garryhinch Oak Tree

Portarlington Golf Club, Garryhinch, County Laois
Quercus robur | **Common or Pedunculate Oak**

HEIGHT: 18m

GIRTH: 8.4m

ACCESS: This tree is located in Portarlington Golf Club which is open to members and visiting golfers.

Golf was first played in Ireland from the mid-19th century, and the first golf clubs were links courses, established along the coast on land which was sandy, windy and treeless. Golf moved inland as it gained popularity among the middle classes around the turn of the 20th century. Soon every large town wanted a golf course, and if they were lucky, beautiful demesnes became available for rent or sale as they were being divided up by the Land Commission. These parkland courses, for which Ireland is justly famed, retained the mature trees as obstacles, between lush tree-lined fairways on gently sloping ground. Golf courses proved to be a haven for old trees, as other demesnes had their trees clear felled for agricultural use.

Portarlington Golf Club in County Laois was founded in 1908 on land leased from the Warburton family at Garryhinch Estate, on the Offaly side of the Barrow River. The featured tree is a common oak by the third green. It is one of the largest maiden oaks in the country, with a stem rising high into the crown to a height of 18m. Maiden trees are single stems which do not fork, or were pollarded out of reach of grazing animals. Its sprouty, burred trunk measures nearly 8.5m, or a bit less because of ivy. I cannot complain as ivy is essential for wildlife, especially as golf courses can be sterile environments. The tree is obviously appreciated, as there is a bench on which to rest tired limbs under its canopy.

Other golf courses renowned for their ancient or champion trees are Headfort, County Meath, Druids Glen and Old Conna, County Wicklow, and the K Club in County Kildare.

One of the largest 'maiden' oak trees in Ireland near the third green at Portarlington Golf Club

Pumpkin Oak at Mote Park

Mote Park, County Roscommon
Quercus robur | **Pedunculate Oak**

HEIGHT: 4m

GIRTH: 7.23m

ACCESS: The tree is located on property owned by Coillte and is open for public access in accordance with the company's open-forest policy.

The pumpkin oak has been sitting forlornly in a state plantation for the last 50 years. It is a remarkable burred common oak in the shape of a giant rounded pumpkin 2.4m high and diameter. The crown was cut off a few feet above the bole, leaving three dead snags resembling Homer Simpson's crown. Over the years the conifers grew taller and left the oak in perpetual gloom and yet the timber did not rot away, but showed the resilience long-prized and used in the great cathedrals and public buildings of Ireland and Europe. There is still life in the form of holly, mountain ash and brambles finding root on top and absorbing the occasional shaft of light that broke through. Three years ago the plantation was felled and the oak now squints its pasty face in the light.

Mote Park is two miles from Roscommon town on the Athlone road and was originally a vast 3,462-hectare estate belonging to the Crofton family. Most of the estate was sold in the early 20th century, and the final nail was driven into the estate in the 1950s and 1960s when the Land Commission demolished the house, felled the beautiful oak woods and divided the remaining land among local farmers. The oak woods were replaced by conifer plantations, and another two pot-bellied hollow oaks struggle to survive beside the road close to the pumpkin oak. Several more oaks survive in a neighbouring farmer's field and one of them at almost 8m in girth is the largest oak in Connaught. Heartbreaking is the sight of equally large old oak stumps tossed into a quarry hole nearby. These bear witness to a destruction that must never be allowed to happen again.

Shaped like a giant pumpkin, the remaining stump of an oak tree at Mote Park

The Hanging Oak with its twisted trunk at Shane's Castle

The Hanging Oak of Shane's Castle

Shane's Castle, Antrim, County Antrim
Quercus robur | **Pedunculate Oak**

HEIGHT: 14m
GIRTH: 6.27m
ACCESS: The tree is located on private property. Viewing is by prior appointment only.

The O'Neills of Shane's Castle are unique in being able to trace their ancestors back at least 1,700 years; these include the legendary Niall of the Nine Hostages. In one story an O'Neill chief cut off his own hand in a race organised to fill the vacant crown, and threw it to the shore, allowing him to claim the kingship of Ulster. The bloodied hand became the symbol of Ulster, and that of the O'Neills. They were Kings of Ulster for a thousand years up to the reign of Elizabeth I and controlled vast territories from their stronghold in Dungannon. In 1230 they divided their lands and the younger brother settled on the northern shore of Lough Neagh at a place called Eden-duff-carraig, which was renamed Shane's Castle in 1722 by a Shane O'Neill. The vast estate between Antrim and Randalstown has always been renowned for its oak forest, and one of the owners was able to pay a fine of £30,000 by felling enough oak trees to pay off his debt. The demesne is now reduced to about 1,052 hectares but it still has the finest collection of ancient parkland oaks in Northern Ireland. A couple of trees felled in the 1980s were ring-counted back to 1649 and 1675. One oak still standing deep in the woods close to the River Main is over 7m in girth and very hollow, and is probably close to 500 years old, making it one of the oldest in Ireland.

Our featured oak stands at a junction of the old turnpike road, which is now inside the estate after it was enclosed by walls in 1847 as a famine-relief scheme. The Hanging Oak may be 400 years old, as it stands with a twisting low trunk with huge limbs growing out and then up like a whirling dervish about to take flight. Those limbs were ideal for throwing a rope over and hanging highwaymen and those who failed to pay the toll for the turnpike road in the 18th century. The arrival of the railway made these roads unprofitable, and by the middle of the 19th century local authorities had taken over their maintenance. I hope no one from the National Roads Authority reads about this tree: it might give them ideas about how to deal with present day toll dodgers!

Ancient Oak at Belvoir

Belvoir Forest Park, Belfast, County Antrim
Quercus robur | **Pedunculate Oak**

HEIGHT: 16m
GIRTH: 8.79m
ACCESS: The tree is located on property which is open for public access during advertised opening hours.

Four hundred years ago Belfast was but a glint in the eye of Arthur Chichester who had just been granted lands around the mouth of the Lagan River. He started a planned town of timber houses, garden plots and an inn, and built a castle of brick on the site of an earlier castle. It remained a small town living in the shadow of Carrickfergus until the end of the 18th century, when it became the centre of the linen industry, and a hub of the industrial revolution, developing rapidly in the 19th century to become the metropolis we know today. This development quickly absorbed large wooded estates such as Malone, Wilmont and Belvoir on the banks of the Lagan, and as a result, Belfast has inherited a wonderful corridor of woods, wildlife and parks along the valley into the countryside. Belvoir Park (pronounced 'beaver'), about three miles south of Belfast, dating from the 1720s and created by Arthur Hill, was one of the largest estates. Gardens, canals and terraces were built before the mansion itself was completed in about 1750. The parkland contained pre-existing oak woodland and fields for grazing. In 1817 the demesne changed hands and became part of the Deramore Estate belonging to the Bateman family. Much of the old woodland was blown down in the great storm of 1839, but the largest tree, called the Belvoir Oak, was still there at the turn of the 20th century, and its girth of 28ft/8.5m made it the largest in Ireland at the time. It was then considered to be over 300 years old, and had been adopted as the family crest.

Since then one half of the estate has become a golf course, while the house and the rest of the estate were sold to a developer, whose plans came to nothing. The Forest Service Northern Ireland took over in 1961 and demolished the house, unfortunately. The remaining 72 hectares now form a forest park. Many large oaks are scattered in the open parkland and woodland, and research shows that some date back to the 17th century. The present Belvoir Oak near the motte bears no relation to photographs of the original, which is presumed gone. But hidden away in the wood is a massive old hollow hulk, shorn of most of its branches and supporting a host of ferns on its decaying trunk. It is called 'Granddad' and is over 8m in circumference. At 500 years old, it could be Northern Ireland's oldest tree. Could this be the original 'Belvoir Oak' in a truncated form, lost and found again?

The ancient Belvoir Oak
at Belvoir Park, Belfast

The Bloody Oak

Bloody Loaming Lane, Salter's Grange, Armagh, County Armagh
Quercus robur | **Pedunculate Oak**

HEIGHT: 18m
GIRTH: 5.1m
ACCESS: The tree is located alongside the public road.

A few miles north of Armagh city and a short distance from the Loughgall road is a quiet country road leading to the church with soaring spire on top of the hill at Salter's Grange. It was close to here that the Battle of the Yellow Ford was fought in 1598 between the British Crown and the last of the great Irish chieftains, Hugh O'Neill, who made a last stand for an independent Gaelic way of life. The English had built a fort by the Blackwater River to help strike at O'Neill's headquarters at Dungannon, and they used an expeditionary force of 5,000 soldiers to relieve the fort after it came under siege by the Irish. It was at the Yellow Ford on the River Callan that O'Neill, in alliance with his powerful neighbour Hugh O'Donnell, defeated and routed the English in what proved to be the last great victory of Gaelic Ireland. They won the battle, but lost the war in 1601 when they attempted to come to the aid of the Spanish fleet, which had been sent to help them, but was besieged in Kinsale by the English. The Irish, led by O'Neill and O'Donnell, were defeated by Mountjoy's English forces at the Battle of Kinsale, and scattered northwards in disarray.

At a road junction near Salter's Grange stands an ancient oak called 'The Bloody Oak', which witnessed soldiers who had fled from the slaughter at Yellow Ford being hunted down and killed under its shade. That lane is called the Bloody Loaming, and the oak stood with an accusing arm pointing towards it, which may have been used for hanging fugitives. The branch remained dead on the tree for hundreds of years, and it was said to have died in protest at having been used for hanging. But the tree lives on, and is so hollow that several people can stand inside it with the nesting jackdaws. Fires have been lit inside the trunk, which seems to have strengthened its resolve to survive and flourish, and it has a good crown despite its great age. This oak may once have been part of the native woodlands of the medieval period. It has seen their destruction and replacement by enclosed fields tilled by generations of men who have come and gone. It is a witness tree deserving of great respect.

The Bloody Oak at Salter's Grange was witness to the Battle of the Yellow Ford in 1598

Roughfort Tree of Liberty

Roughfort, Mallusk, County Antrim
Quercus petraea | **Sessile Oak**

HEIGHT:	23m
GIRTH:	6.19m
ACCESS:	This tree is located on private property but is visible from the Roughfort road which links the B95 and A6 roads.

The Society of United Irishmen was founded in Belfast in 1791 by Wolfe Tone and a group of Catholic and Protestant radicals in order to create an independent Irish Republic based on the French model of liberty and equality. In early 1798, when France offered support for a rebellion, the British government declared martial law and made it a capital offence to take an oath of allegiance to the United Irishmen. The uprising broke out in Leinster in May, and initially had success in Wexford, while in Ulster there was a delay as its leaders waited for the expected French support. The grass-roots supporters grew impatient and elected Henry Joy McCracken as their general. He assembled 25 regiments at the Roughfort Motte, halfway between Belfast and Antrim town. They marched on Antrim in early June, with the intention of capturing its garrison and then using its artillery in the attack on Belfast. It never came to that, as loyal troops just about held on and defeated the 4,000 United Irishmen in what became known as the 'Battle of Antrim', a pivotal event in the collapse of the rebellion in Ulster. McCracken was eventually captured and executed in Belfast in July 1798.

Across the road in a field opposite Roughfort Motte is a majestic solitary oak planted in the 1790s when the United Irishmen planted Liberty Trees as symbols of freedom. Liberty Trees were inspired by a famous elm tree in Boston, named when colonists in 1765 staged the first act of defiance against the British authorities at that tree. Soon other trees were adopted as rallying places of resistance to British taxes in the American colonies. The idea of a Tree of Liberty was also adopted in France following their revolution. The Roughfort Oak is the only original one known to be still standing in Ireland, and it is a terrific example, unmatched by any other in the world. It has a leaning, twisting trunk over 6m in girth, supporting a crown over 30m wide. Locals call it the hanging tree, but there is no record of it being used for such a purpose. To quote Thomas Jefferson, 'The tree of liberty must be refreshed from time to time with the blood of patriots and tyrants.'

The Roughfort Tree of Liberty planted by the United Irishmen during the 1790s

Baronscourt Oak

Baronscourt Estate, Newtownstewart, County Tyrone
Quercus petraea | **Sessile Oak**

HEIGHT: 24m
GIRTH: 8.08m
ACCESS: The tree is located on private property. Viewing is by prior appointment only.

Baronscourt, set in a peaceful valley among the hills of west Tyrone, is one of Ireland's most impressive private estates. This is wild unpopulated country which must have seemed home from home to the three sons of Lord Hamilton of Paisley in Scotland. They were prominent supporters of Mary Queen of Scots, and were granted vast tracts of land in Ulster in the early 17th century. The eldest son, James, was created Earl of Abercorn and it is from him that the present owner of Baronscourt, the Duke of Abercorn, descends. The estate once had 75,000 acres but is now reduced to 15,000 acres of farming, forestry and game-shooting enterprises. The grounds are open occasionally, by prior appointment to various interest groups, and are an incredible window into a way of life from a bygone past.

The main entrance is off the minor road (B84) between Newtownstewart and Drumquin. The estate lies before you like a relief map as you drive down through oak parkland, with Scottish Highland cattle ruminating on their good fortune. Below stands the mansion surrounded by terraced gardens, and beyond is the River Strule which has been dammed to create three glistening, jewel-like lakes. The ground rises again with ancient beech and oak trees scattered on the slopes in quiet contentment.

It is here that the largest and stoutest oak in Northern Ireland is found: it stands by a dirt track that runs parallel to the lake in a deer park. It measures just over 8m around its bulging trunk which seems to be an irritation of corky burrs kept neatly groomed by grazing Sika deer. The healthy crown rises to 24m and demonstrates the typical upright balanced form which distinguishes it from the more rugged and angular form of the common oak. Here in Baronscourt sessile oak has found its optimum growing conditions: high rainfall and humidity on a free-draining, acidic slope. It may not be particularly old at my estimate of 250 years, and with luck it will be around for a long time to come for, as Dryden wrote of the oak:

> Three centuries he grows, and three he stays,
> Supreme in state, and in three more decays.

The largest and stoutest oak tree in Northern Ireland at Baronscourt Estate

Leggy Oak of Moyola

Moyola Park, Castledawson, County Derry
Quercus petraea | **Sessile Oak**

HEIGHT: 36m
GIRTH: 3.2m
ACCESS: The tree is located on private property. Viewing is by prior appointment only.

Moyola Park is a handsome private estate straddling the Moyola River a couple of miles before it enters Lough Neagh. It is the ancestral home of the late Lord Moyola who as Major James Chichester-Clark was the penultimate Prime Minister of Northern Ireland between 1969 and 1971. The house was built in 1768 for the Dawson family who established the small town of Castledawson in the 17th century, which now nestles beside the estate. This is the same family who built the Mansion House in Dublin and gave their name to one of its most prominent streets, Dawson Street.

The long drive up to the house brings one through a magnificent lime avenue and tall sheltering woodlands planted in the 18th century, and opens on to sumptuous parkland with huge specimen trees. One of those trees is Northern Ireland's largest walnut at 4.2m girth and almost 21.3m high. Beyond it is a perfectly proportioned sessile oak 27.4m high with a colossal trunk 6m in girth reaching high into the crown. It is a very rare variety called 'Cochleata' in which the leaves are decurved at the margin, so that the centre is humped or hooded, providing perfect little hats for the squirrels.

Beyond the house a grass path drops down to the Moyola River where tall woods rise up providing shelter to old yews, camellias and magnolia. Walk further on and an array of tall slim sessile oaks reach for the clouds, with clean slender trunks imitating the baleful heron's legs as they eye your disturbing presence. One tree in particular stands out for its chimney-stack trunk glowing in the sunshine without a branch for 21m, with its lollipop crown topping at 36m. Pure perfection! The only other tree to rival it is the 'Squire's Walking Stick' at Tullynally, County Westmeath. I do not know if Thomas Pakenham should see this tree, he might have to concede defeat. There are equally stupendous beech trees in a nearby wood, and they too must have had a forester's care and attention in making them the catwalk models of the tree world.

This oak tree at Moyola Park has a remarkably straight trunk

Turkey Oak of Ballymenoch

Ballymenoch Park, Holywood, County Down
Quercus cerris | **Turkey Oak**

HEIGHT: 27m
GIRTH: 6.67m
ACCESS: Public

Ballymenoch Park is a municipal park beside Holywood which lies above the south shore of Belfast Lough in the middle of County Down's 'Gold Coast'. It earns this sobriquet because it is the most affluent area in Northern Ireland; it is socially divided between the 'haves' and the 'have yachts'. The eight-hectare park is all that remains of the former demesne of Ballymenoch House which burnt down in 1913 after being home to various wealthy merchants since the 1780s. The original grounds of 200 hectares stretched to the coastline, and were bisected by the Bangor road. The park is a pleasant destination with parkland trees and laurel walks, and one truly astounding Turkey oak worth pulling in off the busy road to see.

Turkey oak is native from Turkey to Spain, and along with the holm or evergreen oak is the most common one grown here apart from our two native oaks, the sessile oak and the pedunculate oak. It is the fastest growing of all the oaks, and this tree in Ballymenoch Park will become our largest oak if it lives long enough. It was not planted here until the 19th century.

The Turkey oak is not a good timber tree, as it splits on drying out but its value lies as an amenity tree of great size and presence in parks and hedgerows. It grows well everywhere, and is starting to naturalise in our warming climate, producing lots of seedlings. The biggest trees are in the south-east, with several over 7.5m in girth on private land. The leaves come in many shapes and sizes but tend to be narrower and more lobed than our native oaks. These, along with the distinctive hairy buds and acorn cups, help to identify the species.

The Ballymenoch oak is the largest in Northern Ireland at 6.7m girth and 27m high, with an enormous spread. Unusually for an oak it has a large witch's broom in the crown. Witch's broom is regularly found in birch, hornbeam and Scots pine, and comprises clusters of twigs which look like bird nests, and can be caused by fungi, insects or viruses. The short trunk erupts into multiple stems from about 2.5m up, which support the massive, beautifully proportioned crown that it is much bigger than it looks, and might challenge local golf sensation Rory McIlroy to hit a ball over it.

Northern Ireland's largest specimen of Turkey oak at Ballymenoch Park

The Cork Oak in the grounds of the Church of Ireland at Shillelagh

Close-up of the
characteristically corky bark

Shillelagh Cork Oak

Shillelagh, County Wicklow
Quercus suber | **Cork Oak**

HEIGHT: 10m
GIRTH: 3.13m
ACCESS: Public

Near where I grew up in Palatine, County Carlow, an abandoned walled garden with a cork tree was considered a great marvel. I was told this evergreen tree, with its distinctive thick bark, was unique, and it was hard to imagine how such an exotic tree ended up there. Well, I have had to disappoint many owners when their cork tree proved not to be as unique as they thought with the discovery that there are nearly 70 such trees scattered throughout the country. Their survival here may be down to their resilience. They have to be as tough as old boots considering they get stripped of their dignity every ten years in their native land for the production of cork.

Shillelagh is a pretty little village in south-west Wicklow, historically attached to the coat-tails of the huge Fitzwilliam estate of Coolattin. The name is also given to the Irish fighting stick, mistakenly, as it is really an English transliteration of the Irish '*saol eile*'. The Church of Ireland is perched on a hill commanding wonderful views of the oak woods of Tomnafinnogue and Coolattin, which were sadly depleted as recently as the 1990s.

In front of the church, among the gravestones, stands a lovely spreading cork oak of 3m girth and 10m high. Who planted it, and when, is conjecture, but its size suggests around the time the church was enlarged in 1888. The Wentworth-Fitzwilliam family of Coolattin estate were the main patrons and most likely planters. To be honest, cork oaks are not as handsome as other evergreen oaks, such as the holm oak. The real interest is in its craggy bark and haphazard way of growing, creating the illusion of great age. There used to be a notice in front of the tree asking people not to take lumps of cork as souvenirs.

In Spain and Portugal cork oak forests provide habitats for endangered species, such as the Iberian Lynx and Imperial Eagle. Every time you pop a cork, you are helping a unique environment to survive. May we raise our glasses to that!

Courtown Holm Oak

Courtown Demesne, Courtown, County Wexford
Quercus ilex | **Holm Oak**

HEIGHT: 20m
GIRTH: 13.75m
ACCESS: The tree is located on private property. Viewing is by prior appointment only.

Courtown Harbour is a popular seaside resort on the Wexford coast. In the mid-17th century a large estate was established beside the village by the Stopford family. A local story has it that a Cromwellian soldier by the name of Ford went with an agent to a hill when confiscated land was being distributed. Ford pointed out what tracts of land he wanted, at which point the agent is supposed to have shouted 'Stop, Ford' as the captain was grabbing too much. Today, the big house is demolished and the old estate divided up, but the public can enjoy Courtown Wood along the banks of the Owenvarragh River as it meanders down to the sea. Beyond the wood, the slopes rise up to privately owned fields to where the big house once stood.

In one field stands a small wood which on close inspection turns out to be a single holm oak, sprawling all over the place. Planted before 1648, it is believed to be the first planted in Ireland, and also one of our oldest trees of any species with a known planting date. It only really begins to impress when you crawl under its gloomy canopy. It has multiple stems which fork from the ground, and are partially collapsed as they dip and rise seeking the light. Its girth is an astonishing 14m near the ground.

Holm or evergreen oaks are native to the Mediterranean region, and are the most useful and reliable trees to keep their leaves all winter. They have a brief glorious appearance in June when they shed their dark foliage, and it is replaced by blue-green leaves and golden catkins.

This magnificent Holm Oak at Courtown Demesne predates
1648 and is believed to be the first planted in Ireland

THE ANCIENT YEWS

Yews are the Methuselahs of the tree world. Numerous examples found in graveyards on our neighbouring island of Britain and in Brittany are reckoned to be between 1,000 and 4,000 years old. While there are early accounts of similar ancient trees found at sacred and religious sites in Ireland, none seem to have survived to the present day. We do have a number of trees between 500 and 800 years old, which is not to be sniffed at. These are living monuments worthy of the same protection as the historic buildings found alongside them. Yews were revered in pre-Christian Ireland, and when Christianity replaced the old religion the trees continued to symbolise eternal life. They grow slowly and have the ability to sprout new trunks or even send down roots from high in a hollow trunk, which then become stems replacing the old trunk. Wild trees can still be found around Killarney, on the shores of Lough Derg and inaccessible cliffs in Counties Clare, Sligo, Leitrim and Fermanagh. Most of the large trees we see today were planted on estates in the 18th and 19th century as avenues, shady walks or formal clipped hedges, which have now resumed their natural growth through neglect. Ireland has also contributed two popular cultivars to the botanical world with the yellow-berried yew and the Florence Court or upright yew.

Muckross Abbey Yew

Muckross Abbey, Killarney National Park, Killarney, County Kerry
Taxus baccata | **Yew**

HEIGHT: 17m
GIRTH: 3.09m
ACCESS: Public access during daylight hours.

One of the most celebrated trees in Ireland is growing in the ruined Franciscan abbey at Muckross near Killarney. The yew tree growing in the cloisters of Muckross Abbey has been an object of wonder and awe since the first traveller accounts in the 18th century, and remains so to this day. One Victorian wrote: 'This remarkable tree is preserved with religious veneration by the peasantry, and so awful is the effect produced on the mind by its extraordinary canopy, that many persons shrink back with terror on entering within its precincts, and few can remain long without feeling an impatient desire to escape its oppressive influence'.

The trunk is smooth and straight for 6m before it forks with radiating branches above the surrounding walls. The monks obviously trimmed it so as not to interfere with the adjoining roofs. Various accounts give the foundation of the abbey as 1340 and 1448, and some say that the tree was taken as a sapling from Innisfallen Island and planted at the same time. In 1756 it was described as a tall tree with spreading branches like an umbrella. The top had been cut off, but when the abbey was abandoned by the monks in the 17th century the tree spread and in time overshadowed the whole cloister. There is a legend that the tree was planted over the grave of a monk who had been absent for a hundred years and returned to die. Another story is of a miraculous image of the Blessed Virgin Mary buried underneath, and it was believed that should anyone injure the tree, they would die within the year. This went unheeded by a soldier who hacked off a small branch, which dripped blood. He promptly dropped dead on the spot.

The tree was 6ft/1.8m in girth 200 years ago, and 9½ft/2.9m in 1932. Today it is 10ft/3m and increasing very slowly. There is no simple formula for dating an individual yew as they can deviate enormously from the average, but this tree must be at least 350 years old. Recently during renovations of the Abbey the protective metal cage put around the trunk to protect against vandalism has been removed, allowing for uninterrupted views of the tree. Let us hope that the tree receives the respect it deserves.

An ancient yew tree growing in the cloisters of Muckross Abbey

Burton Hall Yew

Ballynakilly Wood, Burton Hall, Palatine, County Carlow
Taxus baccata | **Yew**

HEIGHT: 19m
GIRTH: 4.3m
ACCESS: The tree is located on private property but is open for public access during daylight hours.

This tree is personal to me. I grew up in nearby Palatine, and the measuring of this tree started me on the quest to record Ireland's champion trees. Its dark brooding presence is found in the middle of a wood north of Carlow.

As one journeys down the straight 'mile avenue' the wood rears up behind the site of the now-demolished big house. The 16 hectares of woodland crown the hill and provide a haven for wildlife among large tillage fields. Perhaps this wood has always been here. It certainly was at the time of Petty's survey in 1650, and hollows and granite outcrops made it unsuitable for reclamation and cultivation. In the 18th century it provided maypoles for May Day celebrations in Carlow town.

What makes the Burton Hall yew special is its enormous trunk rising high into its crown 19m up. It has seen many storms, lost some limbs but still appears to be in its prime. Yews can afford to take the long-term view. This tree's trunk is hollowing out, with a large aerial root coming down and forming a new stem inside the old, renewing itself. This indicates that the trees must be nearly 500 years old. Nearby another old yew was toppled by the 1997 storm yet it has not given up its grasp on life. The branches have reoriented themselves towards the light, forming a new crown. It cannot fall any further, so it may live hundreds more years.

Burton Hall has now reverted to its old Irish name of Ballynakilly. It is open to the public under the stewardship and protection of a trust. Go there on a sunny summer's day and you will just have the hum of insects and the wing-clap of pigeons for company. It is a magical place where time stands still.

A large aerial root forms a new stem inside the old, hollowed-out trunk of an ancient yew at Ballynakilly Wood

Florence Court Irish Yew

Florence Court, Enniskillen, County Fermanagh
Taxus baccata | **Yew**

HEIGHT: 12m
GIRTH: 2.99m
ACCESS: Public during advertised opening hours.

This is the tree that has spawned millions of offspring to be planted throughout the temperate world for their biddable form and clean good looks. Alas, the mother tree is looking the worse for wear, and like the Atlantic salmon after leaving its spawn in a mountain stream, is taking its time to recover its former vitality. It was originally discovered by George Willis, a tenant farmer, around 1760 growing wild on Cuilcagh Mountain on the Cavan/Fermanagh border above the Florence Court estate. What caught his eye was its odd upright form, so he dug it up, and maybe a companion, and planted it in his garden, giving the second to his landlord, Lord Enniskillen, who planted his in his demesne where you can see it today. It is not certain if it was one tree divided or two but George's tree died in 1865.

The Florence Court tree attracted attention after cuttings were distributed to enthusiasts at the turn of the 19th century, and a commercial nursery began selling it as the Irish or Florence Court yew. It was widely available at a reasonable price by the 1840s. What made this variant so popular in graveyards and gardens across the world was its narrow upright crown with no horizontal branches. This made it easy to maintain, and if necessary clip into the desired architectural shape in formal landscaping. Heavy snow can splay branches apart and make it necessary to tie wire around the crown. All yew seedlings start out with the leaves arranged spirally around the stem before the mature stems develop flattened leaves each side of the stem. Irish yews deviate by keeping this spiral arrangement all their lives. The mother yew is female, so all Irish yews, being clones, are also female, but their seeds almost never come true to type, and cuttings are still the only sure way to obtain the upright form.

The mother tree stands in a woodland glade owned by the Forest Service Northern Ireland just outside the National Trust property, and is easily reached by a ten-minute walk. It is healthy enough, if a bit ragged, with bare lower branches covered in moss and lichen. No other tree in the world is more deserving of its sheltered retirement home.

The world famous Florence Court Yew is the mother of all 'Irish Yew' trees

The renowned yews at Crom Castle display a bizarre tangling of branches

Crom Yews

Crom Castle, Newtownbutler, County Fermanagh
Taxus baccata | **Yew**

HEIGHT: 11m
GIRTH: 4.68m
ACCESS: Public during advertised opening hours.

No other trees in Ireland have been subject to more misrepresentation than this pair of yews, floating above the swirling mists of Lough Erne. They are the most feted and best known outside this island, and have been subject to comment since the first account in 1739 by William Henry, who describes the tree as having one trunk of 10ft/3m girth with horizontal branches forming a circular shade, supported by three circles of supporting wooden pillars. No mention of the second tree, and other accounts in the next 150 years have similar descriptions with added information such as that it looked like a giant green mushroom, and that up to 200 people dined under it. Was it a case of 'The Emperor has no clothes' syndrome, or subsequent writers plagiarising previous accounts and never visiting the trees at all? The introduction of photography in Victorian times finally showed two trees, and we all know photographs never lie! We now know that 'the great yew of Crom' is two trees of almost equal size a few strides apart, one male and the other female, whose bizarre tangle of branches drop quickly to the ground having lost their original supports. They have been released from their bondage of being plaited, woven and clipped since the First World War, and new branches have grown up to form a more natural crown almost 12m high.

There are claims that they are Northern Ireland's oldest trees, and may be 800 years old. It seems much more likely that they were planted at the same time as the building of the old Crom Castle in 1611, within the outer enclosed walls. That castle burnt down accidentally in 1764, which left the unharmed trees to become the centrepiece of the old castle ruins and gardens, where Lord Erne used to entertain his guests. Today, Crom Castle estate is open to the public under the stewardship of the National Trust, and nearly 810 hectares of oak woodland, parkland and marshy fringes of Lough Erne are easily accessible. Be sure to visit the most celebrated trees in Ireland, and see what all the fuss is about.

Brook Hall Yew

Brook Hall, 65 Culmore Road, Derry, County Derry
Quercus petraea | **Sessile Oak**

HEIGHT:	13m
GIRTH:	5.28m
ACCESS:	The tree is located on private property. Viewing is by appointment only and a charge of £5.00 per person applies (includes a visit to the arboretum and walled garden).

Brook Hall is a beautiful 18th-century villa overlooking the River Foyle two miles north of Derry city and a mile north of the Foyle Bridge, which is Ireland's longest suspension bridge. The original 17th-century house was the headquarters for King James's army during the famous Siege of Derry in 1689, and was occupied by the Duke of Berwick who commanded the King's army. In 1688 the Catholic King James was deposed, but most of Ireland stayed loyal, apart from a few Protestant enclaves, like Derry, that supported William of Orange. A Catholic army attempted to enter Derry but the gates were shut by thirteen apprentice boys and the city swelled in population by Protestant refugees from the surrounding countryside. King James's army tried to besiege the city and starve the people into submission. A wooden boom was constructed across the Foyle below Brook Hall to prevent ships from relieving starvation in the city. Weeks later, British ships broke through the boom to lift the siege and King James's army melted away.

On a prominent rise above the river is a very old yew tree that bore witness to these events. It stands close to the 17th-century walled garden and at 5.28m girth is the largest in Northern Ireland for a single stem. It could be between 350 and 500 years old and while time and storms have had their impact, it is a grand old tree, with some hollowing and a thinning crown. A story has been passed down in which a French naval officer who died during the siege was buried in a sitting position under the tree.

Brook Hall also happens to be one of Ireland's finest private arboretums, started in the 1930s by Commander Frank Gilliland and continued by his cousin David Gilliland from 1958 to the present day. The arboretum suffered considerable damage in 1961 from Hurricane Debbie, which enabled thinning and replanting and is now renowned for its collection of conifers and tender southern-hemisphere plants. Its national importance is magnified by the planting in the mid-20th century of rare trees and cultivars, when very little planting was done elsewhere. An example of this is the planting in 1948 of the first Metasequoia or dawn redwood in Ireland, shortly after its discovery in China in 1941.

The largest, single-stemmed yew tree in Northern Ireland at Brook Hall

Whimsical Yews at Mount Stewart

Mount Stewart, Ards, County Down
Taxus baccata | **Yew**

HEIGHT: 4–5m

GIRTH: 1.2m

ACCESS: The tree is located on property owned by the National Trust and is open daily for public access (10 a.m. – 4 p.m.) except Christmas Day.

Mount Stewart has to be in the pantheon of great Irish gardens, along with Powerscourt, Illnacullin and Mount Usher, and is remarkable for its diversity of styles. Situated by the eastern shore of Strangford Lough, the estate was established in 1745 by the Stewarts, and it gained protection from the elements by the planting of shelter belts and parkland trees in the late 18th century. The family married into great wealth in the 19th century, becoming very prominent in British social and political life, and were granted the title of Marquess of Londonderry. A sum of £150,000 was spent on enlarging the house, while a meagre £30 was donated for famine relief, despite their Irish estates being greatly affected by starvation. The estate went through a long period of neglect before Lady Londonderry moved back in 1921, describing it as the dampest, darkest and saddest place she had ever stayed in. She wasted no time in removing big old holm oaks from around the house, and creating formal gardens on the grassy terraces. Taking advantage of the mild climate, many exotic trees from the southern hemisphere were planted and integrated into the formal structures. The clipped arches of tall Leyland cypress in the Spanish garden are a remarkable use of this maligned species, while the statuary made by local stonemasons in the Dodo Garden add a touch of humour to the whole experience.

It is in the Shamrock Garden which is surrounded by a 2m-high hedge that our featured tree stands as a centrepiece in the form of a topiary Irish harp. Topiary is the patient art of creating living sculpture in formal or, in this case, whimsical style, and it seems to satisfy the basic human need to control nature. The Shamrock Garden portrays the mythical history of Ireland with another yew clipped into a Fomorian, which was an ancient, mythical race of people. On top of the enclosing hedge the figures tell the story of arriving for the hunt in a boat, shooting a stag, which was saved by the devil, and returning home with just a rabbit! Other examples in Ireland of clipped yew can be seen at Gormanston Castle with the yew tunnel featured in this book, and the clipped parterre in front of Carton House.

A topiary harp of clipped yew in the Shamrock Garden at Mount Stewart

Blarney Castle Yews

Blarney Estate, Blarney, County Cork
Taxus baccata | **Yew**

HEIGHT: 15m
GIRTH: 3.5m
ACCESS: The tree is located on private property which is open for public access during advertised opening hours.

Blarney Castle has a lot more to offer than the hygienic risk one takes by kissing the stone. The gardens and arboretum extend between the castle and house, with magnificent mature trees such as sweet chestnut, beech and western red cedar a real attraction to tree lovers. Interspersed are many rare maples and other species planted in the 1970s and acquired from the famous Hillier Nurseries in the south of England. But it is the Rock Close that should be visited, for its extraordinary cluster of beautiful yew trees growing out of and clambering over the limestone terrace high above the small river.

The exposed rock was augmented with great boulders and other stones in the mid-18th century to create a garden folly of fanciful features such as wishing steps, druid altars and dolmen. Kissing the Blarney Stone certainly lent eloquence to visitors such as Thomas Croften Croker who wrote in 1824: 'It is indeed a fairy scene, and I know of no place where I could sooner imagine these little elves holding their moon-night revelry.' There are over 30 yew trees of between 3m and 5m in girth, which suggests that they were planted at the same time that the folly was created or they may have been incorporated as existing trees for this is a likely site for the natural occurrence of yew. Polished by the scuffling of countless human feet, their exposed, serpent-like roots slither over rocks and through cracks like the giant fig trees of Mayan ruins in Central America. Luckily for us these trees cannot talk for they might be insufferable, living as they do, so close to that stone.

The artistry of nature is seen in the exposed roots of yew trees at the Rock Close, Blarney Castle

Glencormac Yew

Glencormac, Kilmacanogue, County Wicklow
Taxus baccata | **Yew**

HEIGHT: 18m

GIRTH: 6.61m

ACCESS: The tree is located on privately owned property in the garden of Avoca Handweavers Shop/Restaurant and can be viewed by the public during advertised opening hours.

The Glencormac yew has long been thought to be Ireland's oldest and largest yew. Along with the Silken Thomas yew, for many years they were the only ones known to be over 6m in girth. Since the Tree Register was founded in 1999 another three such yews have been discovered.

The earliest reference to yews in Ireland comes from Giraldus Cambrensis who visited here in the 13th century, and mentions that yews are commonly found in sacred places and old burial grounds. Scores of large ancient yews are still to be found in graveyards in Wales and England, but in Ireland they have not been given the same protection. Maybe during territorial disputes and warfare in ancient times, such sacred trees were destroyed as a particularly spiteful form of revenge.

The Glencormac yew can be seen at Avoca Handweavers in Kilmacanogue, beside the N11. Many huge eucalyptus and sequoias dot the grounds. At the bottom of the garden is a 300-year-old yew walk. At its end stands a much larger tree with a magnificent muscular trunk. It looks as if a hundred pythons have collectively decided to build a pyramid. It has been suggested that this tree's proximity to a late 12th-century church indicates that the site was a resting place on the pilgrimage path to Glendalough, where a similar large yew once existed. No real evidence has surfaced for this conjecture.

It was 17ft/5.2m in girth in 1860, and is now about 22ft/6.7m, depending how far above ground it is measured. A dead stump a foot/30cm in diameter taken from the crown contained 170 annual rings. Debate among tree experts on the age of individual yew trees cannot be resolved as they hollow out after about 300 years. My own gut feeling is that this tree is no more than 600 years old. Visit the tree yourself, and its beautiful presence will make all arguments superfluous.

The gnarly, latticed trunk of the Glencormac Yew, one of Ireland's largest and oldest yew trees at Avoca Handweavers in Kilmacanogue

Furness Yew

Furness House, Naas, County Kildare
Taxus baccata | **Yew**

HEIGHT:	17m
GIRTH:	4.5m
ACCESS:	The tree is located on private property. Viewing is by prior appointment only. Appointment to be requested in writing.

Samuel Hayes, whose book *Practical Treatise on Trees* was published in 1794 shortly after his death, is the patriarch of Irish trees and their cultivation. He gave details of around 120 remarkable trees, so for a tree hunter like myself it provided a real challenge to find which of them are still with us some 200 years later. One of his descriptions reads: 'We may see a fine yew … at Fornace, the seat of Richard Neville Esq, in the county of Kildare, the stem, which is very clear for this species of tree, measures 12 feet round at 6 feet high, the branches extend 66 feet, and add much to a pleasing sequestered scene near an old ruin, amidst holly and laurel of extraordinary bulk and great height.'

So 15 years ago I visited Furness more in hope than expectation. Driving up the avenue to be greeted by a magnificent Palladian-style house with two wings set in rolling parkland was promising. Hayes would surely still recognise this, and approaching the church in front of which stands the old yew he would be left in no doubt that its presence has increased in the intervening years. It is now 4.5m in girth, and is no longer quite as tall, but what can you expect after 200 years of exposure to our fickle climate? The rate of increase, if consistent over its whole life, would place it at about 1,000 years old; however, yews are anything but consistent. I would put it between 500 and 700 years old, making it one of the oldest trees in Ireland. The church is probably in a much better state of preservation than it was in Hayes' time. It was an early 6th-century church, built on lands that were bequeathed to the monastery of St Thomas in Dublin after the Norman conquest. The monks extended it in 1210, and eventually it was burnt by Cromwellian forces in 1650.

There are other fine yews, holly and beech in the adjoining woodland, and it would be nice to hope that not much will have changed 200 years from now. Some things are fine just the way they are.

Swiss Cottage Yew

Swiss Cottage, Cahir, County Tipperary
Taxus baccata | **Yew**

HEIGHT: 11m
GIRTH: 5.24m
ACCESS: Public

The restored Swiss Cottage near Cahir is one of the most unexpected and beautiful houses in Ireland. At the beginning of the 19th century, a fashion developed among the gentry for little thatched cottages to be built as a romantic retreat and for entertaining guests. They were inspired by Marie Antoinette and her peasant village at Versailles, where aristocrats played at being peasants and enjoyed simple living.

It is a *cottage orné*; other examples may be seen in Kilfane, County Kilkenny and Derrymore in County Armagh. The Swiss Cottage was built for Richard Butler, Earl of Glengall, who resided at Cahir Castle. It is situated on a limestone outcrop overlooking the River Suir. There are wooded slopes down to the river containing oak, ash and elm with an understorey of hazel, hawthorn and cherry. Exposed limestone pavement runs through, with many large yews growing, and taking advantage of free drainage and scant topsoil, which allows them to compete with greedy neighbours. Yews can survive the axe when it is apparent that other species will not succeed. Similar conditions at Killarney, the Burren and on the shores of Lough Derg have ensured the survival of yew stands elsewhere.

The magnificent old yew beside the Swiss Cottage is 5.24m in girth and has a wide-spreading crown nearly 11m high. The decaying corrugated trunk has descending aerial roots with the long-term strategy of creating a new trunk. In spring, half the tree's crown whitens with male flowers, which shed clouds of pollen. In autumn, the other half is decorated by red berries.

Yew trees are either male or female so its identity crisis reveals that this is actually two trees locked in a romantic embrace. The Cottage was built to complement the tree and that is how it should ever be!

The Swiss Cottage
yew near Cahir

The yew cloisters at Gormanston College

Inside the cloister's tunnels

Gormanston Yew Cloister

Gormanston College, Gormanston, County Meath
Taxus baccata | **Yew**

HEIGHT: 7m
ACCESS: The tree is located on private property. Viewing is by prior appointment only.

Gormanston Castle was the ancestral home of the Preston family from the 14th century up to the 1940s. They were initially a family of traders who, through their wealth and ability to pick the winning side in any conflict, managed to become one of the most venerable families in Irish peerage. They held on to their estates, and were one of the few landed Irish families to remain staunch Catholics.

In the 18th century, a daughter of the family wished to become a nun. This request could have had repercussions for the family at a time when the Penal Laws were enforced, so Lord Gormanston was unwilling to allow her to join a convent. In compensation, he planted the yew walk to represent the cloisters of a monastery, and a beehive-shaped cell for contemplation, also in yew. The daughter must have been elderly by the time it grew into the shape imagined. Generations of clipping has created the remarkable giant green caterpillars we see today. It is only when you enter the triangular tunnel that you can fully comprehend the artistry in creating this living sculpture. You can easily imagine a monk in prayer, or in these more secular times a hairy-footed hobbit hobbling home. The space inside the triangle is taken up by a large cedar, while beyond, towards the graves, are other wonderful exotic trees such as cork oaks and a very fine ginkgo. The family sold the estate in the 1950s, and it became a secondary school run by the Franciscan friars. They have continued to clip and maintain the yews, which used to take all summer. In recent times technology in the shape of a cherry picker has reduced the time needed to five days. Realising how appropriate it is to have a living cloister, they must be commended in looking after this unique heritage for all of us.

Cliff-Face Yew at Turloughmore

Turloughmore Mountain, Glencolumbkille South, County Clare
Taxus baccata | **Yew**

Height:	4m
Girth:	1.1m
Access:	These trees are located on private lands but can be viewed from the Boston to Carron public road, south of Turloughmore.

There is an other-worldliness about the Burren which can be disconcerting to a tree hunter from the rich farmland of the east. It has a combination of land stripped bare and big skies, akin to coming across the bleached bones of a whale on a remote beach. You have to question the sanity of looking for trees in this seemingly lifeless terrain. Was it not Cromwell's deputy in his campaign in Ireland who described the Burren as having not enough water to drown a man, wood enough to hang one, nor earth enough to bury him? But look closer and you will discover that the Burren is a Noah's Ark of vegetation where Arctic and Alpine meet. It is like a giant storage heater with cracks and crevices giving sanctuary to life, in contrast to intensive farming practices. It is with this in mind that one can search for ancient yew trees on cliff faces which are out of the reach of grazing livestock, and inaccessible to the axe and saw. I say ancient because research in recent years in Britain has found yew trees in similar sites with girths not much more than your ankle with 600 annual rings. They are small and stunted because of the harshness of the climate, and as a result of altitude, exposure and lack of soil. Similar conditions produce the world's oldest proven trees, 5,000-year-old bristlecone pines found in the arid regions of south-western North America.

In the Burren many small stunted yews are found on the lower terraces of Mullaghmore. Their dark evergreen foliage is easy to pick out from a distance, but you need to be an experienced rock climber to get close. The privately owned Vale of Clab has a yew with long, exposed roots clambering down the cliff face searching for sustenance. Other cliff-face yews are also found near Belcoo, County Fermanagh and Swiss Valley, County Sligo.

Our featured tree is near the summit of Turloughmore. It is best viewed with binoculars from the road between Boston and Carron, south of Turloughmore, which rises in a series of terraces: the dark green outline of the tree is perched on the eastern end. The altitude and exposure have moulded its shape to hug the cliff like a child refusing to let go of its parent's leg. It is one of my candidates for being Ireland's oldest tree.

Moulded by altitude and exposure, the stunted growth of an ancient, cliff-face yew near the summit of Turloughmore

Reenadinna Yew Wood at Killarney National Park – this natural yew wood is unique in Ireland and one of only three in Europe

Reenadinna Yew Wood

Killarney National Park, Muckross, Killarney, County Kerry
Taxus baccata | **Yew**

HEIGHT:	12m
GIRTH:	2m
ACCESS:	Public during advertised opening hours.

Reenadinna is a unique 40-hectare yew wood found in the temperate rain-forest of Killarney National Park. Pure yew woodlands are found in only a handful of places in Europe, and the character of Reenadinna differs from them in the abundance of lichens and moss due to the high rainfall and humidity. The wood has a dense canopy, which makes it a dark, almost eerie place. The wood is found on the peninsula which separates Muckross Lake and Lough Leane, a short walk from Muckross House. It is restricted to the limestone rocky outcrops that were laid down about 300 million years ago during the Carboniferous Period, when this area was submerged under a warm shallow sea. Limestone is soluble, which has resulted in grykes or channels forming, which allows enough soil to build up for yews to germinate and grow. Yews have a preference for well-drained, lime-rich soils and here have become the dominant tree, with their dense shade and ability to outlive other species seeing off the competition. The wood escaped the clear-felling which occurred elsewhere in the Killarney area in the 18th and early 19th centuries. But there are no really large, ancient trees which would indicate a continuous yew wood; most trees appear to be the same age and size, and there is no regeneration due to grazing by Sika deer and other herbivores. Other tree species, including ash, holly, whitebeam and arbutus, occur on the fringes, while downy birch and alder are found in wet hollows. Elsewhere in Ireland, yew is found occasionally in mixed woodland where it has self-seeded on similar limestone pavement, or been planted. In the yew wood the ground flora is limited by shade to hart's-tongue and soft-shield ferns, while the soft green moss covers tree trunks and boulders like a beautiful carpet. Tread softly as this mystical wood is unique not just in Ireland but in the world.

OTHER NATIVES

Ireland has been an island for about 11,000 years since the sea rose to separate us from Britain, which was cut off from continental Europe much later. Some species did not have a chance to migrate to Ireland from their refuge in southern Europe, although the arbutus or strawberry tree is found here and not in Britain and its presence here is still a mystery. What all this means is that Ireland has far fewer natives that arrived here naturally than Britain, which in turn has far fewer than across the channel in France. Of the trees featured in the following pages, the ash turns up time and again. It is the dominant tree of our landscape, and there are more monumental ash trees here than in the rest of Europe. The potential loss of these trees to ash dieback disease is just too tragic to contemplate. Scots pine is also well represented, even though it is thought to have died out before being reintroduced from Scottish and European seed. The inclusion of a white willow and a black poplar in this section may be challenged by some experts, as their status as natives is disputed, some classifying them as introductions. One of the most common native trees of all, namely the hawthorn, is covered later in the book.

Ballynatray Ash

Ballynatray Estate, Youghal, County Cork
Fraxinus excelsior | **Ash**

HEIGHT: 15m

GIRTH: 8.45m

ACCESS: The tree is located on private property and is generally not open for public access. For more information visit website: www.ballynatray.com

Living as I do near the River Barrow, it pains me to admit that the Munster Blackwater may be the most scenic river valley in Ireland. The Ascendancy certainly knew the value of prime real estate, and their wooded demesnes have largely survived intact along the banks of the Blackwater. Continuity of ownership has ensured the management of woods and parkland, and the pressure to convert such land into the prairies that has prevailed elsewhere has been resisted here. Native and exotic trees that were planted extensively to enhance the picturesque scenery still survive and make the valley a hotspot for champion trees.

Ballynatray House is perfectly situated, overlooking the last bend before the Blackwater spills into Youghal Bay. The newly restored gardens are open during the summer months. You enter the estate over a causeway spanning the Glendine tributary. To your right are the ruins of a medieval abbey, while the rising ground to your left is an old deer park. One low squat ash tree stands alone, seemingly indifferent to the glorious views it commands. It is only when you get close that it materialises into Methuselah himself. It is a cave with branches sprouting above the nibbling line of cattle. Its gnarly trunk is a lattice of holes and bumps defiant against the storms that try to topple it. Even the branches are hollow as you peer up from inside the trunk. It has so many nooks and crannies that the contents of Noah's Ark could be rehoused in it.

Ireland is still a land of giant ash trees and I have recorded at least 70 with a girth over 6m. This tree, at almost 8.5m girth, is the biggest daddy of them all, and perhaps the oldest at an estimated 400 years. Two hundred years is a good age for an ash, while 300 would be exceptional. Walter Raleigh used to own these lands, and luckily for us he did not make a pipe out of this ash when it was just a sprig.

One of Ireland's largest and oldest ash trees at Ballynatray Estate

Crannabachall Lookout Tree

Coolaghmore, Callan, County Kilkenny
Fraxinus excelsior | **Ash**

HEIGHT:	19m
GIRTH:	5.32m
ACCESS:	The tree is located on private property but is visible from the adjoining public road R698 between Callan and Windgap.

On a twisting road between Callan and Windgap stands a huge rugged ash tree inside the neatly clipped hedge of a bungalow's front garden. It commands views over the countryside and approaching roads and is one of the few living links to a dark period in our history.

In 18th-century Ireland all existing churches had come under the control of the established Protestant state. Penal Laws were passed preventing Catholics from voting, holding office or buying land, and while not prohibiting the worship of their religion as such, priests had to take an oath of allegiance to the Crown or suffer persecution. The reward for the capture of a priest flouting the oath was £10, and fugitive priests had to be careful as they carried out secret ceremonies. Irish Catholics had to celebrate Mass on primitive altar tables in ruined churches and other secret outdoor places, because there were no churches for them.

One such place is at Coolaghmore where a Mass Rock was situated a quarter of a mile from our featured tree, named Crannabachall, which appropriately translates as 'the shepherd's hook tree'. It was a lookout tree from which someone reliable would warn the priest and congregation of any approaching strangers during the Mass. The ash tree is still 19m high above the road and over 5.3m in girth, and is covered in ivy and probably hollow. When it is bare in winter you can see the shepherd's hook in the crown's outline. It seems to be at least 300 years of age, if not more. There was a second lookout tree a mile down the Callan road, but it is long gone. Next time you travel this road please salute this remarkable survivor and wonder if trees could talk, what stories this one could tell.

Commanding views over the surrounding countryside, the Crannabachall ash tree was used as a lookout during penal times

The Tree That Ate the Church

Tihilly Church, Laughaun, Coleraine, County Offaly
Fraxinus excelsior | **Ash**

HEIGHT: 20m
GIRTH: 7.18m
ACCESS: The tree is located on privately owned property but public access is permitted to view the tree.

I have been as guilty as anyone in rushing through the countryside on our improved road network, and not seeing some of the wonders of our beautiful island. The road between Tullamore and Clara was one I had often travelled, when a beam of sunshine illuminated a pair of ash trees I had not noticed before. They are two fields in, behind a farmyard, and after getting permission from the farmer I approached them with growing anticipation. Surface roots of the first ash seemed ready to grab my ankles and pull me into its gaping cavity. The gargantuan tree did not look benign and, if I did not know better, appeared to be 'Old Man Willow' exiled from Tolkien's Middle-earth. It stands on a mound of stones which are the remains of Tihilly church. Moss-covered stones and bark merge to create a trunk 7.6m in girth, a new Irish champion at the turn of the millennium. Since then its cavity has become a cave, which has shrunk its girth to 7.18m. It supports a respectable storm-damaged crown, and at over 300 years old, is living on borrowed time. It probably started life as an opportunist seedling on the walls of the church, when it was abandoned in medieval times. Two walls remain standing beyond its grasping roots.

The second ash stands proudly clear of all this carnage, and is in the prime of life, ready to guard this religious site when the old brute is gone. It shelters a standing High Cross made from sandstone, which depicts scenes from the Bible, along with geometric and animal interlacing. St Fintan founded a monastery here in the seventh century. The last abbot served here in 936, while the church we see now was built from the stones of previous churches.

Ash trees have a special place in Irish folklore, and massive old trees have been venerated down through the ages. After the hawthorn, it is the tree most likely to be found at holy wells and sites of special significance. Here we have a tree to rival those of the past and I hope to revisit it before it returns to Middle-earth.

A mound of stones at the base of this hollowed-out ash tree is all that remains of Tihilly Church

The Great Ash of Tynan Abbey displays a most impressive trunk measuring over 7m in girth

Great Ash of Tynan Abbey

Tynan Abbey, Tynan, County Armagh
Fraxinus excelsior | **Ash**

HEIGHT:	24m
GIRTH:	7.19m
ACCESS:	This tree is located on private property and is not open for public access.

Tynan Abbey is part of a triumvirate of great wooded estates which live cheek by jowl in this quiet corner of Ulster. Partition in 1922 divided Castle Leslie in Monaghan from Caledon in Tyrone, and Tynan Abbey in Armagh, the border literally running along the walls between them. Gateways and bridle paths unite them, along with a great passion for planting trees which have survived to the present, making this one of the great tree hotspots in Ireland. The 'Troubles' had the effect of battening down the hatches for Caledon, while Castle Leslie reinvented itself as a family-run hotel. Tynan Abbey suffered grievously when, in one of the worst atrocities by the Provisional IRA, the former MP Sir Norman Stronge and his only son, James, were murdered in the library in Tynan Abbey in 1981, and the house burnt down. The unstable structure of the ruin was demolished in 1998, and today Sir Norman's descendants live in the stable-yard complex and the place reverberates to the sounds of children again.

The parkland has the up-and-down topography of drumlin country, with streams and ponds feeding the lush pastures among colossal 18th- century-planted trees. One of the great trees is the tallest oak yet measured in Ireland at 38m. Another oak at 7.6m girth is one of the largest in Northern Ireland, and there is a line of 12 sweet chestnuts in deep woodland along the disused Ulster Canal, which must have been planted at its completion in the 1840s. Tynan Abbey is best known for its giant ash trees, with the largest at over 26ft /8m in girth, and in 1976 reckoned to be the finest ever seen by the late Alan Mitchell, the renowned botanist and forester, but it fell in the 1980s.

Waiting in the wings was another ash which has now taken centre stage. It is a superb tree with a 3m-high cylindrical trunk and very even, vertically ridged bark. Even though it is now over 7m in girth, it is unlikely that in time it might become even larger than the previous champion, as it is very hollow, with an opening that foxes used as a den now large enough for a calf to shelter in. It stands on a great pedestal of roots, which prevent cattle from getting too comfortable under its light shade. Ash trees are precautionary weather vanes with the country rhyme of:

> Oak before the ash and there will be a splash,
> Ash before the oak and there will be a soak

The Doss Tree

Portlee West, Toome, County Antrim
Fraxinus excelsior | **Ash**

> **HEIGHT:** 13m
> **GIRTH:** 4.32m
> **ACCESS:** The tree is located on private property but is visible from from Cargin Road, which is a public road intersecting with the Shore Road, south of Toomebridge.

The townland of Doss lies by the northern shore of Lough Neagh at Toome-bridge, where it narrows into the outflow of the River Bann. The Doss Tree is the only tree, apart from the Royal Oak in Killarney, to be marked on current Ordnance Survey maps, and has been consistently so since the first maps of the 1830s.

Locally it is known as the Cabin Tree as the remains of many houses lie just under the surface nearby, and show that there was a considerable pre-Famine population in the area. The Doss Tree is a mighty and battered old ash which has had its main stem snapped off 6m up with three large branches turned up like the sails of a windmill waiting for the breeze to send them twirling. It stands between a country boreen and the shore, and in a landscape of pasture, low hedge and water, it is one of the most striking landmark trees in the country. The trunk is knobbly and bulging on the outside, while inside is an enclosed cave with holes for windows. Scattered on the ground lies the debris of storms past, untouched by human hand for fear of the fairy folk, and the bad luck from burning the dead branches. The tree benignly allows a couple of ropes to hang loose for local children to swing on, and their laughter must surely lull the devil himself to sleep. Down through its 300 years, the Doss Tree has been a marker for fishermen to use in alignment with the nearby Artlone Hill to set their nets and be able to find them again.

It is also a witness tree to meetings of insurgents during the 1798 Rebel-lion, and in quieter times cockfights were held under its boughs. It has seen famine and disease wipe whole communities from the district, and stood mutely while fishermen battled to earn a living. Through it all Lough Neagh laps close by, but even the lough is threatened by the demands of a thirsty nation.

The Doss Tree has been used for over 300 years as a marker
by fishermen on Lough Neagh (in the background)

The Saffron Hill Pines

Saffron Hill, Doneraile, County Cork
Pinus sylvestris | **Scots Pine**

HEIGHT: 35m

GIRTH: 3.16m

ACCESS: The tree is located on public property but access is through adjoining lands in private ownership. Directions and permission for access to be sought by calling to adjoining house.

'They shoot trees, don't they?' is a paraphrase that springs to mind when one thinks of the Saffron Hill pines near Doneraile. Doneraile is a pretty village on the Awbeg River among the fertile pastures of north Cork. It was a planned town, created in the early 18th century to serve the needs of the vast Doneraile Court estate. If you travel to the top of the village, the New Road brings you along the southern walled perimeter of the demesne. Soon the wooded slopes of Saffron Hill loom up on your right. The wood is owned by Coillte, but access to it is through private property, so please seek permission.

The name Saffron Hill comes from the presence of yellow crocuses, whose pollen stigmas were used to dye clothing centuries ago. Once inside the 13-hectare wood, you are met with venerable oak trees, and have to squelch through an undergrowth of giant laurels to get to the treasures in its depths. Beware of darkness falling, for there are stories told of a ghostly Lord Doneraile with spectral horses and hounds still hunting for that elusive fox. Rather more alarming are reports down the ages of a giant ostrich roaming about.

What brings us here are two Scots pine which may be the last of their kind. Ireland was once covered in large pine forests, which are thought to have been destroyed by early Christian times. Historical records refer to the survival of some trees in remote parts of the country.

H. M. Fitzpatrick, in his report to the 1933 Conifer Conference, states: 'At Doneraile Court there is a group of fine pines growing in an oak wood on Saffron Hill, which local tradition affirms to be from the seed of Irish pine collected in Kerry. These trees are of great age, and are remarkable for their smooth bark.' Fitzpatrick measured the largest at 12ft/3.6m girth, and the two that remain now are 10ft/3.1m and 11ft/3.4m in girth, with the taller at 114ft/35m, being one of the tallest in Ireland. Both have beautiful straight stems high into the crown without a branch. Samples of foliage and cones need to be taken for genetic testing, and compared with foreign Scots pine but they are well out of reach, and such precious trees do not need a tree climber damaging the lovely bark on the way up. The solution comes from the practice of the early collectors, who used guns to shoot cones and foliage out of trees hundreds of feet high to send them to the botanical institutions in Europe.

So to answer the initial question: yes, they do shoot trees!

Scots pine tree at
Saffron Hill

Scots Pine at Doo Lough

Doo Lough, Sheeffry Hills, County Mayo
Pinus sylvestris | **Scots Pine**

HEIGHT: 16m

GIRTH: 1.5m

ACCESS: The trees are located on private property but are visible from the R335 public road, known as the Doo Lough Pass.

Doo Lough is arguably the most scenic spot in Ireland. The name comes from the Irish meaning 'black lake' and is a valley and pass squeezed between Mweelrea Mountain and the Sheeffry Hills in south Mayo. Words fail to convey the epic beauty of the still lake surrounded by the green and russet slopes, with cloud shadows skipping through on sunny days. The grandeur of this lonely Eden is tainted by a dark and terrible tragedy that occurred here during the Great Famine of 1845 to 1849.

In March 1849, the famine had reached its peak and the people of Mayo had suffered more than most. The British government decided to let market forces solve the problem by importing Indian meal and slowly releasing it to maintain its price. The starving population were expected to earn money in public works rather than depend on handouts. Only the poorest, with less than a quarter of an acre, were entitled to claim poor relief. On that fateful day, when such relief was being given out, they were told to face inspection to claim 3 lb of meal in Louisburgh, ten miles north of Doo Lough. The two inspectors left instructions for the 600 starving people to follow on foot to Delphi Lodge, two miles south of Doo Lough, where the Inspectors themselves were being entertained and where the people would be inspected the following day. The living skeletons walked the 12 miles south by the lough to Delphi only to be hit by a storm which resulted in the deaths of countless victims. The callousness and inhumanity of the inspectors increased when they denied the survivors relief, and ordered them back to Louisburgh. At that time the only trees to bear witness to this calamity were the fine beech and sycamore around Delphi Lodge. There were no trees around Doo Lough until after 1851, when another hunting lodge called Dhulough House was built at the south end of the lake, and a woodland of Scots pine was planted. They have grown slowly and elegantly into the iconic trees that frame photographs beside the little pier at the lake. They look so right in this landscape and really they have come home, as Scots pine was the dominant tree species in this area in prehistoric times. The picture would be complete if eagles or ospreys were to take up residence here. Stop and listen to the keening wind rush through the trees and mourn the tragic dead of Doo Lough.

Scots pine are an integral part of this iconic landscape at Doo Lough

Coronation Plantation

Manor Kilbride, County Wicklow
Pinus sylvestris | **Scots Pine**

HEIGHT: 15m

ACCESS: These trees are on privately owned land but can be viewed from the R759 public road linking Manor Kilbride to the Sally Gap.

A favourite route into the Wicklow Mountains for Dubliners is to take the road to Blessington. Turn left at Kilbride and follow the road to the Sally Gap as it rises with the River Liffey to its source under Kippure Mountain. Near the top a signposted trail to the right brings you to the Coronation Monument. It is a granite obelisk which honours the accession to the throne of William IV in 1831. Before you stretch mountain meadows in mellow shades of golden brown and drifts of purple heather. A scene of big skies and desolation is interrupted by windswept Scots pine in scattered groups and lone trees. If you are quiet, deer may be seen grazing to complete the picture. It resembles what it must have been like in prehistory when Scots pine grew on our hills before climate change and human interference banished them from our landscape.

Scots pine, along with juniper and yew, are our only native conifers. They are found throughout Europe and Asia, all the way to the Pacific Ocean. Scots pine established itself in suitable habitats throughout Ireland soon after the ice age ended. It had disappeared by early Christian times so that it had to be reintroduced from Scottish seed in the 18th century.

The Downshire estate owned vast tracts of land between Sally Gap and Blessington, and this plantation was begun in 1831 as a local forestry development. Larch, oak and poplar were also planted but fared poorly on the peaty slopes. Some of the trees were felled in 1912, and forest fires had an impact so that the mature trees you see today look so right, so natural. Look over your shoulder at the regimented blocks of Sitka spruce on the slopes of Kippure. I know which I prefer.

The Coronation Plantation of Scots pine near the Sally Gap named in
celebration of the coronation of King William IV in 1831

Scots pine line both sides of the Frosses Road between Ballymena and Ballymoney

The Frosses Pines

The Frosses, Ballymena, County Antrim
Pinus sylvestris | **Scots Pine**

HEIGHT: 17m
GIRTH: 1.5m
ACCESS: These trees are located alongside the A26 public road between Ballymena and Ballymoney.

Trees may be planted by roads for many reasons, including landowners screening their property from the public, or just embellishing the landscape. In India the Grand Trunk Road is renowned for its centuries-old fig trees planted for shade, but this is certainly not the reason for the handsome pine trees along the Frosses Road between Ballymena and Ballymoney. They were planted in 1840 by Charles Lanyon, who was County Surveyor and an engineer constructing the new Antrim-to-Coleraine Mail Coach Road. The Scots pine were intended to support the road as it was laid on a bog, and have formed a guard of honour for travellers ever since. Some 1,500 were originally planted but the ravages of time and the health and safety concerns of the local authority have reduced their number to fewer than a hundred. The present road does not meet the requirements of modern heavy traffic, and the trees have been under threat of removal for some time as the road cannot be widened without their destruction.

Many young trees have been planted as replacements, and now form a substantial hedge half the height of the leaning, older trees. It may be another hundred years before they shed their lower limbs, and take on the flattened tops of their seniors. What make these much-loved landmark trees unique is that the two lines lean uniformly and inwards towards each other over the centre of the road. This is probably due to the road footings gradually sinking into the bog, and bending the trees towards the middle. It is hoped that the Frosses Road will be bypassed, and the present stretch will be retained as a lay-by, so that we may admire the trees without putting our lives at risk and contemplate the words of the poem 'Pine-Trees and the Sky: Evening' by Rupert Brooke (1887–1915):

> Then from the sad west turning wearily,
> I saw the pines against the white north sky,
> Very beautiful, and still, and bending over
> Their sharp black heads against a quiet sky.
> And there was peace in them, and I
> Was happy, and forgot to play the lover,
> And laughed, and did no longer wish to die,
> Being glad of you, O pine trees in the sky!

Scots Pine at Baronscourt

Baronscourt Estate, Newtownstewart, County Tyrone
Pinus sylvestris | **Scots Pine**

HEIGHT: 28m
GIRTH: 4.4m
ACCESS: The tree is located on private property. Viewing is by prior appointment only.

Apart from the eternal yew, no other conifer species has more resonance in literature than the Scots pine. This may be because of it being omnipresent in northern latitudes where winter introspection lends it magical qualities. Even on a winter's day its crown looms dark and brooding, suspended on patterned trunks which glow in pink and orange in the low sunshine. Unfortunately, through climatic change and their destruction by human intervention, the once-widespread pine had disappeared from Ireland's landscape by early Christian times. It had to be reintroduced in the 18th century, when it found a new home on large estates such as Baronscourt. The Dublin Society (now the Royal Dublin Society) was so concerned about the scarcity of good commercial timber that grants were given to improving landowners, and we can see remnants of those plantings, especially of Scots pine, in County Wicklow. But the problem with Scots pine is what is known as 'a facile snare for the uninitiated'; that is, the pine is easy to raise and establish on a wide range of soils and sites including some of the most difficult, but there is always another forestry species which will outgrow it, and yield more.

One of the finest Scots pine stems in Ireland may be seen at the magnificent Baronscourt Estate in deep woodland by the largest of its three lakes. Planted in the 18th century, it became submerged in more recent western hemlock plantations and was lost from view and forgotten until the woods were thinned, and the pine rediscovered 20 years ago. Its clean cylinder stem of over 3.8m girth rises more than 18m before its first branch, but even this tree demonstrates 'the facile snare', for a Sitka spruce would attain the same dimensions at a third of its age. An even greater pine in a more open situation is found beside the pleasure grounds, where exotic trees and shrubs are sheltered by scattered pines in what is called the flower wood garden.

This Scots pine is seen through a gap in the vegetation on the right before the pleasure grounds. At over 4.4m girth, its trunk is the largest single stem in Ireland and rises high into its domed crown with a few dead snags to give the tree an air of great age and presence. This is one pine that does not have to justify its continued existence to any forester.

The largest-girthed, single-stem Scots pine in Ireland, over 4.2m girth, at Baronscourt Estate

The 'Haunted Bush' by the Old Bog Road, Connemara

Haunted Bush by the Old Bog Road

Old Bog Road, Connemara, County Galway
Crataegus monogyna | **Hawthorn**

HEIGHT: 2m
GIRTH: 0.38m
ACCESS: This tree is visible from the R341 known as the Old Bog Road, from Roundstone to Clifden.

There is an 11km stretch between Cashel and Clifden in west Connemara called the 'Old Bog Road'. The road winds its way through a desolate land-scape of stone, bog and lake with nothing but the occasional sheep and the plaintive call of the curlew for company. This is no place to be caught out in the elements and back in the 19th century there was a hostelry called the Half-Way House which was a convenient stop for travellers and people walking home from fairs. Today, there is no habitation for miles around, and it is easy to pass the stone ruins of the former inn without noticing, as it merges into the rocky background. The other side of the road has a lone windswept hawthorn bush, no taller than a man, in splendid isola-tion, trimmed by hungry sheep. It is here where the story begins, although I cannot vouch for its authenticity, as it may have gained wings in inter-vening years.

Stand at the bush and look south as the land drops down to Lough Agaddy just over half a kilometre away. In the middle of the lake is an island covered in furze. This was home to a thief who preyed on travellers at the inn. He would first select a victim by making sure they were alone with no friends or family nearby. He would dispatch his victims close to the lone bush, and bury them in the bog on his retreat back to the island. He used a half barrel to float over and no one was able to follow. The Half-Way House closed a hundred years ago and the people who passed through have been forgotten and crumbled into dust – or have they? Look towards the lake: a scattering of holly and mountain ash are believed to be the reincarnation of those murdered souls, their blood rising annually in the red berries. Recently an old man has been seen sitting beside the hawthorn bush at the oddest of times. Could he be a traveller from another dimension?

Champion Willow at Deerpark

Deerpark, Dublin Road, County Carlow
Salix alba | **White Willow**

Height: 19m
Girth: 6.3m
Access: The tree is located on privately owned property but may be viewed by the public from the adjoining public road, the R448 Dublin Road, formerly the N9.

The magnificent white willow on the Dublin Road had a companion willow on the opposite roadside until recently. It was cut down before anyone could shout 'stop'. I called them portal trees, framing the entrance to Carlow. Trees like this are most at risk from road widening and development. I hope this book will help protect and cherish them.

White willows are plentiful along the rivers and drains of the midlands and south Ulster. They look as if they belong but it is thought they were introduced a millennium ago. In Britain they are regularly pollarded for poles and the production of cricket bats. In Ireland its tough light timber was used to make harps, of which the medieval 'Brian Boru' harp (on display in the Long Room in Trinity College Dublin) is the best example. The tree in Carlow is over 6m in girth and very hollow, before erupting into an enormous multiple-stem crown from 2.1m above ground. Many people fear a tree is doomed when hollowed out but any structural engineer will tell you that a tube has greater strength and flexibility than a solid rod. Nature has provided a way for trees to extend their life. Seed is viable for only a short time, but they have a trick up their sleeve. Twigs may drift downstream and lodge in the riverbank. Try it yourself and push one into damp ground. Roots soon develop and in the blink of a year or two you have a fast-growing tree. Willows go by the maxim of 'live fast, die young'. The Carlow tree is an exception, and might be all of 150 years old. The long narrow leaves are covered in silky white hairs giving them a blue-green luminosity in the breeze. Stop by this tree on a summer's day and admire the shimmering crown against the blue sky. It is an Impressionist painting come to life.

Ireland's largest-girthed white willow alongside the old Dublin Road out of Carlow

A uniquely woven root system forms the base for this
fine specimen of common alder at Legan

The Legan Alder

Legan, County Longford
Alnus glutinosa | **Common Alder**

HEIGHT: 11m
GIRTH: 5.82m
ACCESS: This tree is located on private property but is visible from a small, unmarked road off the N55 (the Athlone to Edgeworthstown Road). Very difficult to find.

Alder is normally associated with streams, rivers and drains where there is movement of water to keep the oxygen level high. The land around Legan in south County Longford is a mixture of rich grassland and raised bog. So to find one of Ireland's oldest and largest alders in the middle of a pasture, with no apparent running water nearby, is a bit of a mystery at first. When you get up close the mystery deepens, for the trunk is not solid; it is, rather, a tree on stilts of its own roots. I have been assured that the tree still exists, and that it is not a figment of my imagination. The landscape might be the clue, as I think that the field was drained and dropped in level by a couple of feet. This left the alder high and dry, standing on its own roots like a mangrove tree at low tide. The new trunk now looks as if it was created by a basket maker with a woeful hangover. Its girth of 5.8m is only exceeded by a couple of trees in Killarney National Park and another in the Uragh, also in Kerry.

In the distant past, during the Bronze and Iron Ages, alder was the preferred timber for making shields, and examples in the National Museum show that enormous trees were selected. No trees exist today with such dimensions. The common alder is most appreciated by birdwatchers, as it is in a class of its own as a source of seeds for birds, especially finches, in winter. The alder is also a great defence against erosion of riverbanks. Alders are best seen in late winter when emerging twigs and catkins glow in the sunshine.

Tower Wood Strawberry Tree

Tower Wood, Killarney National Park, Killarney, County Kerry
Arbutus unedo | **Strawberry Tree**

HEIGHT: 10m
GIRTH: 3.21m
ACCESS: Public. Access during daylight hours.

The arbutus or strawberry tree is unique among our native trees in being the only species found in Ireland that is not native to Britain. The arbutus is presumed to have migrated from north-west France before the ocean swamped a land bridge at the end of the last ice age. It is restricted to areas where the mean January temperature is above 5 °C, so that it is now found in south-west France and around the Mediterranean. In Ireland it was probably much more widely distributed, from Waterford to Cork, and up the west coast to Sligo: place names such as Cappaquin, Quin and Quinsheen Island, all names derived from *caithne*, the Irish word for arbutus, indicate previous haunts. Today it is found naturally only at Lough Gill in County Sligo, Killarney and Sneem in County Kerry, and Glengarriff in County Cork.

The strawberry tree is remarkable in simultaneously bearing its creamy-white, urn-shaped flowers alongside the ripening fruits in autumn

The arbutus is a member of the heather family, and distantly related to heathers and rhododendrons, but it can tolerate limy soil. It is an evergreen shrubby tree which flowers in drooping white clusters in autumn, at the same time as the small strawberry-like fruit ripen from the previous year's crop. The bark is a dull red-grey, while the pink timber was so coveted by charcoal and furniture makers that its very survival was threatened in times past. It will thrive in limy or acidic soil, providing it is free-draining and not shaded by other trees. In its Killarney stronghold, it is most common by the rocky shoreline of the lakes. The arbutus reaches its greatest size in Killarney, and many of the finest can be seen between Muckross and Dinish Cottage, where some are 12m high with single stems up to 2.4m in girth.

Our featured tree and champion is much bigger, older looking and gnarlier than any other tree. It can be seen in Killarney beside the road tunnel on the way up to Moll's Gap beside the Upper Lake. Every other arbutus is a shrub in comparison to the wonderful knobbly and hollow trunk which forks at head height. It is about 3.2m in girth and supports a broad crown 10m high, which unfortunately appears to have lost most of its evergreen leaves in the few short years I have known it. Arbutus has the ability to re-sprout from the base, and may potentially live several hundred years but I fear this noble tree's days are numbered and soon we may have to seek a new world champion elsewhere.

Cinnamon-coloured flaking bark on the trunk and branches of Ireland's largest-girthed strawberry tree at Killarney National Park

A magnificent specimen of black poplar on the shores of Lough Allen

Lough Allen Black Poplar

Organic Galloway Farm, Lecarrow, Drumkeeran, County Leitrim
Populus nigra | **Black Poplar**

HEIGHT: 23m

GIRTH: 6.8m

ACCESS: This tree is located on privately owned property but is visible from a slipway at the end of a public boreen (unnamed and unnumbered) off the R280 at Lecarrow.

Next time you drive along the western shore of Lough Allen, slip down to the pier at Lecarrow. A little further along the lakeshore stands the daddy of all black poplars. The crown is as broad as its height of 23m. Almost 7m in girth, the trunk has many of the knotty burrs so beloved by woodturners. The tree has the typical leaning, rugged trunk with branches upswept before arching over pendulously at the tips. Black poplars are even easier to find in winter once you recognise their profile. They are native throughout Europe but have become very scarce due to an inability to reproduce naturally, and being replaced by faster-growing hybrids. In Britain only about 2,000 mature specimens are to be found. In Ireland close to a thousand are known from Lough Allen down through the Shannon river system, across the midlands to the Liffey, and on to the river valleys of the south-east. Black poplar's status as a native tree is under debate. Most botanists regarded it as introduced, but it has a very natural distribution in river systems and floodplains. Few are found in demesnes and other man-made plantings. Trees of mixed age indicate that the population is stable and regenerating. More research needs to be done as our trees could be of international importance. They are majestic trees in our landscape and should be planted more often than the boring faster-growing hybrid poplars.

Holly at Glenveagh

Glenveagh, County Donegal
Ilex aquifolium | **Holly**

Height: 10m
Girth: 2.2m
Access: Public

Glenveagh National Park lying deep in the Donegal Highlands encompasses 30,000 hectares of mountain, lake and bog, with a 19th- century castle and gardens as the focal point of this wilderness. The land was bought and the estate created by John Adair, a successful land speculator who had done well in America and returned to Ireland with the intention of creating a hunting estate to rival the royal estates in Scotland. He gained a terrible notoriety by evicting 244 families whose cabins spoiled his view, which he did not enjoy for long, as he died suddenly in 1885, a dozen years after the castle's completion.

The gardens we see today are largely the vision of his American widow, Cornelia, who created them over the next 30 years. Twelve hectares were fenced off from the introduced red deer herd, and Scots pine with rhododendrons planted for shelter. A one-hectare lawn was reclaimed and levelled from a bog, and many tender species from Australasia and South America planted to frame the sylvan setting in a Robinsonian style seen in other famous Irish gardens. Native trees such as oak, aspen and mountain ash are mixed in to complement and pull the composition together.

Another underrated native is our featured tree in the form of a large, twin-stemmed holly perched above the lawn. This particular holly shows just what the species can achieve in about 120 years, if left to its own devices and not harvested annually for its Christmas berries. It is 10m high and 2.2m in girth which is not bad for a so-called shrubby or understorey species. Other hollies around the country have reached 21m, and the sprouty remains of a holly on Innisfallen Island in Killarney survive from a tree that was over 4m in girth 220 years ago, which would make it at least 400 years old. Hollies are either male or female, and need a mate for berries to be produced, which can begin within six years from being a seedling. They are a valuable food source in the winter for birds whose droppings often disperse the seed in inaccessible places such as cliffs and the forks of other trees. The Glenveagh tree shows its smooth pale bark to advantage and the glittering prickly leaves show that it can hold its head up in any company.

A native holly tree at Glenveagh

Elderberry Throne at Temple House

Temple House, Ballymote, County Sligo
Sambucus nigra | **Elder**

HEIGHT: 3m
GIRTH: 0.95m
ACCESS: The tree is located on private property. Viewing is by prior appointment only.

The Knights Templar were a monastic order founded in the 12th century to take up arms to protect the recently captured Jerusalem, and to escort pilgrims to sites in the Holy Land. They came to Ireland after the Norman invasion and were established in Dublin and Munster before building their most westerly stronghold at Temple in County Sligo in 1216. Ireland was a long way from their original purpose, but they recruited knights, owned large estates and were responsible for ensuring that taxes arrived at the English court safely. Their financial clout led to their downfall, as they lent vast sums to the king of France, Philip the Fair, who was unwilling to pay his debts. In 1307 Philip had the Templars arrested and tortured, and he confiscated their fortunes in France. He had control over Pope Adrian, and the Templars were soon doomed throughout the rest of Europe.

The castle at Temple by the River Owenmore was granted to another Crusader order, the Knights Hospitallers, and went through various Norman and Gaelic owners before the present Perceval family married into its ownership in 1665. They lived there until 1760 and moved into a new house built in the classical style a short distance uphill. Since then the castle has been slowly crumbling, with huge sections falling to create a graveyard of scattered ruins. One of these sections looks like a giant throne with a small gnarly elderberry growing from its seat.

You may wonder how an elder merits a place in a book about trees when it is cursed by gardeners everywhere for its shrubby weediness, and its ability to seed anywhere. I have measured some up to 15m high and 2.5m in girth. Mature old specimens like our featured tree have lovely creamy, corky bark with criss-cross ridges, and are an adornment to our hedgerows with their creamy plates of flowers in May. Elderberry wine comes from the black berries, which ripen in August and, although poisonous when raw, they have many medicinal uses. This elder sitting on its throne must be the King of the Trees in the same way as the wren is the King of the Birds.

A mature elderberry nestling within the throne-shaped remains of a 13th-century castle at Temple House

Weeping Elm at Rathmullan House

Rathmullan House, Rathmullan, County Donegal
Ulmus glabra 'Pendula' | **Weeping Wych Elm**

HEIGHT: 6m

GIRTH: 3.3m

ACCESS: The tree is located on property which is open for public access during advertised opening hours from mid-February to late December.

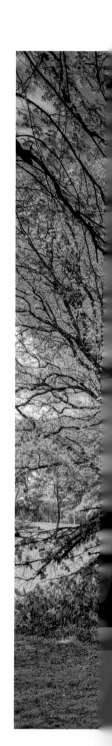

In the cool summers of the north of Ireland, Dutch elm disease has spread slowly, and has left Donegal as the last stronghold of mature elm trees still surviving. But even here as at Rathmullan House Hotel every year brings new losses, and soon generations of tree lovers to come will never know the glory of the elm in our landscape. The wych elm is the only undisputed native elm in Ireland, although the Cornish elm found in Munster and Brittany is accepted by some experts as native. Wych elm has the most northerly distribution in Europe and is never injured by late frosts, so that its fertile seed is produced in abundance. It also never suckers, which helps distinguish it from other elm species. The leaves tend to be larger than on other elms, and the crown arches up and then over to create a broad dome. They once were the largest tree of all in our native forest with some measured to 36.5m high; a famous tree in St Wolstan's, Celbridge, County Kildare was toppled in 1776 when it was almost 12m in girth. The earliest Neolithic farmers 5,000 years ago knew their value as indicator trees of soil fertility, and felled them in large numbers to create fields for their crops. Elms are renowned for their malicious bad tempers as Rudyard Kipling wrote in 'A Tree Song':

> ... Ellum she hateth mankind, and waiteth
> Till every gust be laid
> To drop a limb on the head of him
> That anyway trusts her shade

This should not be a problem with our featured tree on the front lawn of Rathmullan House by the shore of Lough Swilly. It is a weeping wych elm that is only 6m high, with large horizontal branches stretching 9m out from its short thick trunk and then weeping at its tips like a giant's table covered with a cloth of leaves. Weeping elm is a cultivar grafted on a regular elm's rootstock and originally came from Scotland in the early 19th century. Another weeping elm died recently nearby while there are several conventional wych elms in the well-maintained gardens of the hotel. See them soon before it is too late, or you will just have my word that these unique trees ever existed at all.

Weeping Wych Elm at Rathmullan House

THE
EUROPEANS

This section of the book consists of trees from Britain and
Europe, which were introduced to these shores by humankind.
Some such as the hybrid elm may have arrived thousands of
years ago, introduced to our flora by the first farmers. Others such
as beech, sycamore, lime and hornbeam were first planted here
about 400 years ago as useful windbreaks, and to beautify the large
demesnes which were created out of our ravaged and denuded land.
These trees are so ubiquitous and naturalised that it is hard to believe
that they were once exotic. Southern European species such as sweet
chestnut and walnut with their useful fruit have not quite escaped
the confines of gardens and estates, but with a warming climate may
become established in our hedgerows and woodlands, with the
help of grey squirrels and rooks. Other species like silver fir, horse
chestnut and Norway spruce add variety to our tree palette,
and must make migrating birds and insects feel right at home
as suitable habitats for wildlife being forced northwards by
rising temperatures. These immigrants are looked down
on by some native woodland conservationists but our
landscape would be much poorer without them.

Nuns' Graveyard Beech

Díseart, Dingle, County Kerry
Fagus sylvatica Atropurpurea Group | **Copper Beech**

HEIGHT: 13m
GIRTH: 3.68m
ACCESS: This tree is located on public property and may be accessed during advertised opening hours.

Significant trees can appear anywhere, but out on the Dingle Peninsula, facing the wild Atlantic, still seems an unlikely spot. The Presentation Sisters founded St Joseph's Convent in 1829 in the town of Dingle, at the request of the Bishop of Kerry, and soon established a school for girls. This was a time of Catholic emancipation when restrictions were lifted on the Church following the repeal of the Penal Laws and the failure of the 1798 Rebellion. In the 1860s the nuns gave part of their garden for the construction of the new Church of St Mary's, and also had to remove their graveyard as it was at the rear of the new church. It was soon afterwards that the present nuns' graveyard was established, and the copper beech planted. The convent eventually closed but since 1998 the convent and grounds have become the home of Díseart Institute of Irish Spirituality and Culture. Many visitors come to see the 6 two-panel windows by Ireland's most renowned stained-glass artist, Harry Clarke, in the nuns' former chapel.

A short walk will take you to a corner of the gardens where a broad sweeping copper beech stands guard over the exquisite and simple grave-yard. Dozens of small, white iron crosses stand in orderly ranks, enclosed within a white fence under a canopy of delicate beech leaves in shades of pink, purple and crimson, depending on the time of year. If the oak is the king of trees then the beech must be the queen, as it is the most graceful in the curve of its branches and smoothest in texture of its crown. The copper and red tones of the leaves bring to mind the blood of Christ in this tranquil resting place.

In Europe when copper beeches appeared occasionally in the wild they were rumoured to be the mark of nature's disapproval of some unnatural crime. This did not stop copper beeches becoming popular for their contrasting hues and, if planted in moderation, they can be very effective in the landscape.

The broad canopy of this copper beech tree overhangs the nuns' graveyard in Dingle

Beeches at Monaincha Abbey

Beeches at Monaincha Abbey

Monaincha Abbey, Roscrea, County Tipperary
Fagus sylvatica | **Common Beech**

HEIGHT:	22m
GIRTH:	5.07m
ACCESS:	Public

Monaincha Abbey is one of the most picturesque ruins in the country, and it is found off the Dublin road just outside Roscrea. Turn down a narrow lane and walk the final approach across a large field. Go there on a sunny morning with a mist blanketing the fields, and it may become the most enchanting meeting with trees in your life. Monaincha translates as 'island of the living', and the abbey is situated on what used to be an island in a bog. In the 18th century the bog was drained and the perimeter of the sacred mound was marked by a retaining stone wall. The spectacular beech trees were planted in a circle around the ruins.

The monastery is linked with the sixth-century St Canice and the eighth-century St Elair. Texts from Giraldus Cambrensis' 12th-century description of Ireland and the 14th-century Book of Ballymote describe Monaincha as the 31st wonder of the world, and report that no man ever died there. However, any woman or female animal died as soon as they set foot on the island. I wonder which abbot thought that one up to keep the monks from distraction?

The six remaining beech trees bookend the 12th-century Augustinian church, and appear to have the same texture and colour as the carved stone they shade. They have multi-stemmed forks at head height, and huge buttresses down to the ground mirroring the branches above. They resemble the giant fig trees found on Mayan ruins of Central America.

Bective Abbey Beech

Bective Abbey, Kilmessan, Trim, County Meath
Fagus sylvatica | **Common Beech**

HEIGHT: 22m
GIRTH: 4.52m
ACCESS: Public

Bective Abbey is now in a farmer's field close to the River Boyne in County Meath. It was built in 1147 by King Murchad of Meath for the Cistercian monks, and was one of the most important monastic sites in Ireland. It was heavily fortified and following the dissolution of the Catholic Church by Henry VIII in the 16th century, it became a manor house, and was abandoned soon after to become the magnificent ruin we see today.

Its appeal to the photographer's eye comes from the presence of a large, handsome beech tree that acts as a counterpoint to the hard architecture. These days we tend to view landscapes through the frame of a camera lens or car window, and it amuses me to see photos of houses in the property pages with a branch of a tree thrust into the foreground. Every tree is precious to somebody, and trees are our umbilical cord to the natural world viewed through a window at work or home. We must be vigilant for the sound of a chainsaw or the revs of a bulldozer. A 500-year old tree can be felled in five minutes, and what we take for granted is gone forever. It is comforting to know that this tree is appreciated and protected.

The Bective Abbey beech tree is as finely proportioned a specimen as you will see anywhere. It fills a corner of the enclosed ruin with its 22m spread and height,

and its girth of 4.52m suggests that it was planted in the late 19th century. Beech is also our most reliable tree for autumn colour. Unfortunately most of the beech trees we see now were planted in the 19th century, and are very mature and vulnerable to the next big storm. In a book about heritage trees maybe I should just whisper it, but it is the best of firewood. Shush!

The Bective Abbey beech against the backdrop of
this 12th-century monastic settlement

The Duke of Leinster Beeches
at the Moat of Ardscull

The Duke of Leinster Beeches
form a dominant backdrop in
this rolling landscape

Beeches at Moat of Ardscull

Moat of Ardscull, Athy, County Kildare
Fagus sylvatica | **Common Beech**

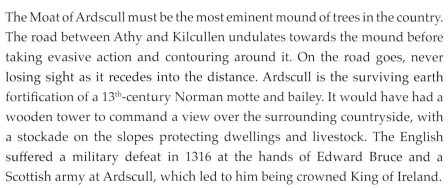

HEIGHT:	20m
GIRTH:	2.5m
ACCESS:	National Monument visible from R448 between Athy and Kilcullen.

The Moat of Ardscull must be the most eminent mound of trees in the country. The road between Athy and Kilcullen undulates towards the mound before taking evasive action and contouring around it. On the road goes, never losing sight as it recedes into the distance. Ardscull is the surviving earth fortification of a 13th-century Norman motte and bailey. It would have had a wooden tower to command a view over the surrounding countryside, with a stockade on the slopes protecting dwellings and livestock. The English suffered a military defeat in 1316 at the hands of Edward Bruce and a Scottish army at Ardscull, which led to him being crowned King of Ireland.

The moat quietly slipped from the pages of history, and no stone structures were built to rival the visual acclaim of the Rock of Dunamase a few miles away. It became the abode of the little people (or 'gentry' as they prefer to be known). A fairly reliable source tells the story of a hunchback who in passing the Moat one evening heard bagpipe music and singing from the summit. He looked in to find a large gathering of the gentry singing 'Monday, Tuesday' to which the hunchback added 'Wednesday', which delighted the throng. They offered him a favour, which caused his back to straighten. News of this cure reached another hunchback who impatiently shouted 'Thursday, Friday' to the air when he burst in on their singsong. Rage ensued, which led to the previously discarded hump being added to his own, and he was sent packing amid shouts of laughter.

In the 1820s the Duke of Leinster, who did not need permission from anyone, planted the mound with beech trees. A retaining wall was constructed at the base of the mound which completes the splendid sight we have today. Ardscull, which translates as 'hill of shouts', has a pleasant walk through the skinny grey trunks of the beech wood, and is enchanting in autumn when the child in all of us can kick amber leaves for fun. Just be careful what you shout for, as you-know-who may be listening.

Demented Beeches at Parkanaur

Parkanaur, Dungannon, County Tyrone
Fagus sylvatica var. *tortuosa* | **Contorted Beech**

HEIGHT: 4m
GIRTH: 1.71m
ACCESS: Public during advertised opening hours.

Parkanaur is a forest park a few short miles west of Dungannon, where the M1 narrows into the A4 on the way to Enniskillen from Belfast. The large Gothic Revival house was built for the Burges family around 1850, and most of the parkland trees, woods and pleasure grounds date from this period. The estate was sold in the 1950s and the house reopened as an education centre for young people with special needs in 1960. The grounds were opened to the public in 1983 as a forest park. Parkanaur is home to a unique herd of white fallow deer that graze in an enclosed area of parkland. They are descended from a herd in Mallow Castle in County Cork which were a present from Queen Elizabeth in the 16th century. Close to the house the pleasure grounds contain many fine specimen conifers and rhododendrons with an exotic champion *Lomatia* from Chile being a highlight.

Under the shade of a large oak appears the unimpressive sight of two green mounds of leaves. They are *Fagus sylvatica* var. *tortuosa*, commonly called parasol or twisted beeches, and it is only when you walk under their canopy that you can see why I call them demented. They are mutated freaks in the corkscrew twisting of their branches which eventually bend over and droop to the ground. They were planted here in 1880 after being discovered in a wood nearby when they were already 1.8m high and possibly 50 years old. They are now 4m to 4.5m high and twice as broad, which is pretty slow growth for trees that are nearly 200 years old.

In Europe about 1,500 mature contorted beech trees are found in clusters in a line from Brittany through northern Germany into Denmark and southern Sweden. One theory is that a radioactive meteor may have caused their genetic mutation centuries ago. In south-west Sweden there is a small wood of contorted beeches called the 'Troll Forest'. It is said that malicious trolls one night came and twisted the trees for fun, but soon got tired and returned to the mountains in the north. Is it possible that one of the fairy folk had a similar impulse one night in Parkanaur?

Corkscrew twisting of the branches of the contorted beech at Parkanaur Forest Park

Wesley Chestnut at Rossana

Rossana, Ashford, County Wicklow
Castanea sativa | **Sweet Chestnut**

HEIGHT: 19m
GIRTH: 10.78m
ACCESS: The tree is located on private property. Viewing is by prior appointment only.

The Rossana estate next to Mount Usher in Ashford was the home of the Tighe family from the early 18th century. The same Tighes also owned Woodstock in County Kilkenny, which makes them among the great planters of exotic trees in Ireland. Rossana (formerly Rossannagh) still has some of the finest sessile oaks to be found anywhere and a couple of ancient yews stand guard on a prehistoric mound. But pride of place must go to a remarkable sweet chestnut tree. It was planted in 1718 and was a substantial tree when the preacher and founder of Methodism, John Wesley, visited in 1789. Prayer meetings were held in the house while he is reputed to have preached to assembled crowds under the tree. A painting from much later and a stone plaque under the tree commemorates the event.

What is indisputable is that it has the greatest girth for a broadleaf tree in Ireland. In 1903 it was 29ft/8.8m around its waist, and is now over 35ft/10.7m, and a modest 62ft/19m high, and has become stag-headed with crown die-back. The gnarly trunk forks into three massive branches from about 8ft/3.4m and looks identical to an early photograph taken in 1859.

Sweet chestnuts are also called Spanish chestnut or breadfruit trees, and originate from the Mediterranean. There are many old rugged trees scattered over the country, with many bigger than the largest oaks. A feature of such trees is that their ridged bark assumes a spiral that broadens with age.

There are many other so-called Wesley trees in Britain and Ireland, under which he preached, and he certainly knew the power and imagery created in people's minds at such gatherings. He chose well in selecting this wonderful chestnut to continue his legacy.

Ireland's largest-girthed broadleaf tree – the Wesley chestnut at Rossana measures over 10.7m

The Armada Tree

St Patrick's Church, Cairncastle, County Antrim
Castanea sativa | **Sweet Chestnut**

HEIGHT: 10m
GIRTH: 4.85m
ACCESS: Public

The Spanish Armada was a fleet of 130 ships that sailed from La Coruña in August 1588 to escort an army from Flanders that aimed to invade England. A storm and an attack by English navy fire ships split the Armada apart and drove 110 ships into the North Sea. The ships, many of them damaged, attempted to sail around Scotland and Ireland in order to return to their home ports in northern Spain. Their navigation was poor, and they were ill-prepared for the conditions of the North Atlantic which resulted in up to 25 ships being wrecked off the Irish coast from Antrim to Donegal and down the west coast to Kerry. Most of the survivors were massacred, while others regrouped, as in the case of two wrecked ships on the Donegal coast whose sailors were picked up by the galleon *La Girona* which sailed back towards Scotland, where they could count on the help of their Scottish allies. The rudder broke, and the ship ran aground off Lacada Point in north Antrim which resulted in the loss of 1,300 lives and left only five survivors.

Perhaps it was one of those lost souls who was washed ashore and found on the beach below Cairncastle at Ballygally, a few miles north of Larne. Local folklore tells of the Spanish sailor being buried in St Patrick's Churchyard in Cairncastle in an unmarked grave. One of the edible chestnuts in his pocket germinated to grow into the ancient tree that marks his grave today.

If this is true then the tree would be the oldest with a known planting date in Ireland. The tree is rather small at 4.85m in girth for a species that grows large just about anywhere, even in a windswept graveyard a long way from its home in southern Europe. It has a gnarly leaning trunk supporting twisted branches which have been lopped in the past, preventing it from outgrowing its allotted space. It is a beautiful tree with an extraordinary tale. We leave it with the thoughts of the poet Celia Thaxter (1835–1894):

> Spanish women, over the far seas,
> Could I but show you where your dead repose!
> Could I send tidings on this northern breeze
> That strong and steady blows!

(From *Among the Isles of Shoals*, Boston 1873)

The Armada Tree at St Patrick's Church in Cairncastle tells an extraordinary tale

The Twelve Apostles at Oakfield Park

Oakfield House Demesne, Raphoe, County Donegal
Castanea sativa | **Sweet Chestnut**

HEIGHT:	18m
GIRTH:	9.89m
ACCESS:	The tree is located on private property. Viewing is by prior appointment only. For more information visit website: www.oakfieldpark.com

Oakfield Park was built in 1739 for the Church of Ireland Dean of Raphoe, and subsequently sold in 1869 to a Captain Butler-Stoney who expanded it and turned it into a country estate. In 1998 after a number of owners and a period of neglect, the house and gardens have had a loving restoration by the Robinson family and is now open to the public during the summer months. It was well-timed for tree lovers visiting Donegal, as Ardnamona beside Lough Eske with its magnificent rhododendrons and conifers, is no longer open to the public.

Thousands of trees have been planted to enhance the mature parkland trees which frame an oval lake and Croaghan Mountain in the distance. Many of the trees appear to be as old as the house and the first horse chestnut on your right between the house and the lake looks older than Methuselah himself. It has an extraordinary hollow trunk that a horse could pass through, and it seems only the bark is holding the large crown up, defying gravity and logic. The trunk now measures 5.79m but it must have been much larger as so much of the trunk is now gone. A pole is propped under a vast horizontal branch in what seems to be a placebo rather than having any real benefit, but still it stands. Close to the lake is a sweet chestnut with a lovely spiral ridged trunk with large burrs hanging on like a bad case of haemorrhoids. (Actually, the nuts when ground down were used as a country remedy for haemorrhoids in Europe, and gypsies used to wear nuts around their necks to prevent this affliction.)

Our featured tree is another sweet chestnut a bit further on, and when you see how it erupts in a multitude of trunks from the ground, the reason for the 'Twelve Apostles' moniker becomes apparent. Half of those trunks have had their heads lopped off, leaving large stumps, but it is still a grand tree and is almost 10m in girth near the ground. It is an apt tree to plant on church or convent grounds because in Christianity the sweet chestnut tree symbolises goodness, chastity and triumph over temptation, because of the prickly covering of the nuts.

The multi-stemmed 'Twelve Apostles' sweet chestnut at Oakfield Park

The Cranmore Chestnut

Cranmore, Malone Road, Belfast, County Antrim
Castanea sativa | **Sweet Chestnut**

HEIGHT: 23m
GIRTH: 7.15m
ACCESS: The tree is located on private property. Viewing is by prior appointment only. Contact the Registrar.

Today the ruined house of Cranmore and its abandoned gardens stand among the playing fields of Royal Belfast Academical Institution which are on the Malone Road, to the south of the city centre. It seems incredible that the oldest house in Belfast should be so uncared for and unappreciated, and that its restoration is not given priority. It was built for the Eccles family in the early 17th century during the Plantation of Ulster, and it was here in 1690 that William of Orange rested and tied his horse to a tree during a rainstorm on his march from Carrickfergus to the banks of the River Boyne, where he would forever leave his mark on Irish history. After the Battle of the Boyne, the house was named Orange Grove. At the turn of the 19th century it was renamed Cranmore House, from the Irish for 'big tree', by John Templeton, who is often referred to as the father of Irish botany. Templeton was born there in 1766 into a prosperous merchant family, which allowed him to indulge in his passion for natural history and plants. It is most likely that some of the trees on the property today were planted by him. Inspired by the French Enlightenment, he was an early member of the United Irishmen, but became disillusioned after the occurrence of sectarian murders. He died in 1825, and the following description comes from J. C. Loudon, writing in 1837: 'All the trees at Cranmore except the chestnut and the oaks, were raised from seed by Mr Templeton ... The dimensions sent include a chestnut of sixty feet high and 15 feet in circumference (the tree from which the place takes its name).'

Today there are two very large old sweet chestnuts in front of Cranmore House. The larger is 7m in girth, and a mighty fine old hulk it remains. But is it the same tree that has seen so much history? Well, it seems that supporters of the King William Tree have taken a leaf out of the rag tree book, and adopted an adjacent tree when the original fell in a storm. Research by Ben Simon, Belfast's man of trees, has revealed that the present King William Tree is the third tree to succeed the original, but we should think no less of it for that, as it is a remarkable tree in its own right.

A sweet chestnut at Cranmore House, birthplace of renowned Irish botanist John Templeton (1766–1825)

Adam and Eve Hanging Trees

Ballyraheen, Tinahely, County Wicklow
Castanea sativa | **Sweet Chestnut**

HEIGHT: 16m
GIRTH: 5.87m
ACCESS: This tree is located on privately owned land but is visible from the Shillelagh to Tinahely public road, the R749.

Many times I have driven between Tinahely and Shillelagh. On one side are gentle, gorse-covered hills dotted with sheep. On the other side, at Tomnafinnoge, is the finest sessile oak woodland in Ireland. Word came to me that a hanging tree by the roadside was to be found at Ballyraheen. In a case of not seeing the wood for the trees, I had never noticed it before. There it was, by a large field of barley. How could I have missed it? Sweet chestnut can remain incognito until their moment of glory in midsummer when they are festooned with creamy flower catkins. They are native to the Mediterranean and were probably introduced some 500 years ago. Prized for their nuts, they need hot summers to produce chestnuts fit for roasting. Faster growing than oaks, they become with age our gnarliest, largest broad-leaf trees.

Once inside the field, this tree shows its great age. It has a writhing, twisting hollow trunk while close by is Eve, a dead stump, and Adam's partner in love and crime. Up high in the crown a huge horizontal branch hangs over the field. Perhaps this gives credence to local folklore that the trees were used to hang sheep rustlers in the times before transportation sent desperate people out of sight and mind. Nearby over a hundred people lost their lives in a skirmish in the 1798 Rebellion. Another story is of kindling collected from the trees then burnt in the fireplace, which resulted in a well turning sour. Whatever the truth, the trees are left well alone. Considering how in those times sheep were valued more than people, I wonder if rustlers were hanged as a warning to others, or to allow sheep to count in their sleep, undisturbed.

Hanging tree alongside the road between Shillelagh and Tinahely

Hornbeam at Dunganstown

Dunganstown Castle, Kilbride, County Wicklow
Carpinus betulus | **Hornbeam**

HEIGHT: 19m

GIRTH: 5.79m

ACCESS: The tree is located on private property. Viewing is by prior appointment only.

Nestling among the coastal hills south of Wicklow town is a small church and fortified house at Dunganstown. A Georgian house, with a clutter of farm buildings surrounded by fields of corn and sheltering trees, completes the pastoral scene. Just out of earshot, the constant stream of traffic on the N11 passes by unknowing and without care. An 18th-century yew walk connects the house to the church, while two single yews are found near the castle. Those two yews were referred to by Samuel Hayes in 1794 as being 'remarkable for their form and being mostly six feet round'. Today, they are 14ft (4.2m) round, and their form, with corrugated trunks, is still remarkable. Nearby, the long-gone Hodgins Nursery supplied trees and shrubs to the great estates over 200 years ago. Many holly cultivars still popular today originated there.

Beside the house is a hornbeam of astonishing dimensions. The wonderful fluted bole rises up in a mishmash of columns supporting a vast, healthy spreading crown. Alice (Elsie) Henry, widow of the famous plant collector Augustine Henry, measured the tree in 1941 and found it to be 17ft 6ins (5.3m) in girth. It now measures 19ft (5.8m). Its slow increase in growth suggests a tree of great age, and it is my candidate for being the oldest exotic tree in Ireland.

Hornbeam can be mistaken for beech, but close inspection shows the leaves to have serrated edges, while the male flowers hang in catkins in spring. Like the beech and the lime, hornbeam never made it to Ireland before the post-glacial land bridge was washed away by rising seas. Britain remained connected to Europe long enough for those species to get a foothold. While no showstopper, they are modest pleasant trees, which turn a lovely yellow then gold, and finally orange in autumn.

The remarkable trunk of the
hornbeam at Dunganstown Castle

Silver Fir at Avondale

Avondale Forest Park, Rathdrum, County Wicklow
Abies alba | **Silver Fir**

HEIGHT: 45m

GIRTH: 6.02m

ACCESS: The tree is located on property owned by Coillte and is open for public access in accordance with the company's open-forest policy.

For most people, Avondale is renowned for being the birthplace of the great 19th-century nationalist leader, Charles Stewart Parnell. The Parnell family inherited the estate from our main protagonist, Samuel Hayes, when he died in 1795. Samuel Hayes was a barrister, and member of the Irish Parliament for County Wicklow. Planting trees was his passion, and his book, *A Practical Treatise on Planting*, was the first book on trees in Ireland. He hoped the book would inspire people to love trees, as well as being a guide to planting and managing trees. He also described and recorded notable trees in Wicklow, and neighbouring counties. Several of those trees are still alive today. One could say that he was the father of Irish trees and forestry. Symmetry was achieved in 1904 when the state bought Avondale and its 360 hectares to establish a school of forestry, and plant experimental plots of many species which are still of great importance to the practice of silviculture in Ireland.

A few oak, yew and a magnificent sweet chestnut still survive from Hayes' planting in the 18th century. The finest of all, though, is a colossal silver fir, which may be seen down by the river, after winding through groves of spruce, Douglas fir and redwoods. There was a companion fir nearly as big, which died a few years ago. You can now enjoy uninterrupted views of the giant after a recent clear-up. It is 45m high and over 6m in girth, and as big as any in its native Central European mountain ranges. The main trunk reaches high into the crown, with large lateral branches suddenly turning up with big elbows, creating a candelabra appearance. Silver firs were the tallest trees in Ireland until they were overtaken by American species of spruce and fir about 70 years ago. They are seldom planted now, which is a shame, as their rugged character will be missed.

Giant silver fir at
Avondale Forest Park

Tallest Broadleaf in Ireland

Borris House, Borris, County Carlow
Populus x *canadensis* 'Serotina' | **Hybrid Black Poplar**

HEIGHT: 44m

GIRTH: 5.4m

ACCESS: This tree is located on private property but is visible from the public pathway along the River Barrow.

The River Barrow became navigable over 200 years ago, and features a combination of towpath, locks, canal and river. The lower reaches of the river are spectacularly scenic, as it squeezes through a wooded gorge, between the Blackstairs Mountains and Mount Brandon. Pull in by Ballyteigelea Bridge, which crosses the river between Borris and Graiguenamanagh. From there walk a mile downriver on the towpath to Borris Lock. Slowly but surely, you will glimpse an immense tree looming above the oak woods in the distance, and when you pass the weir you are almost there. It is the closest thing to one of Pandora's home trees from the film *Avatar* that you will find in Ireland. It is a hybrid black poplar nearly 44m high, making it the tallest broadleaf tree in Ireland. The trunk is almost 5.5m in girth, without any apparent taper to its first branch at 21.3m. The upswept branches create a goblet-shaped crown touching the clouds. In the 18th century the eastern cottonwood introduced from America hybridised spontaneously in Europe with the native black poplar. Several different cultivars were selected to make huge trees with their vigorous growth and long clean stems. I think this cultivar is called 'Serotina', which means 'late into leaf', and is a male so it does not shed cotton seeds. I may be proved wrong, as there are many similar hybrids and back-crosses, making identification difficult. It is flourishing in the damp alluvial soil by the river, and may be no more than a hundred years old. See it now before the next big storm does its worst, and enjoy one of the most charming walks to visit a tree in Ireland.

Ireland's tallest broadleaf tree at 44m high is this hybrid black poplar at Borris House

The Duleek Lime

The Green, Main Street, Duleek, County Meath
Tilia x *europaea* | **Common Lime**

HEIGHT: 17m
GIRTH: 6.49m
ACCESS: Public

A wonderful, huge common lime tree dominates the village green of Duleek. It appears to be in the prime of life, and its clean fluted trunk belies its impressive age. But this tree is only a youngster compared to some of the thousand-year-old limes which still survive in Central Europe. Many of those are up to 15.2m in girth, and are propped-up caves; they prove this tree's potential to live a long time yet.

The tree dates from the time when William of Orange and Mary accepted the throne of England in 1688, supplanting King James II, who fled to France and took refuge with Louis XIV. The conflict was resolved two years later at the Battle of the Boyne. The lime and an ash were originally planted and entwined to represent William and Mary. The ash was still there when Oscar Wilde's father, Sir William Wilde, author of *The Beauties of the Boyne and the Blackwater,* visited in 1849, but it has since died. The lack of buttressing on one side suggests the former ash's position.

In 1783 a man called Austin Cooper described a unique custom: 'On the green stands a large tree under which the freedom of the town is given by taking the person who receives that honour and bumping his rump against the tree, to which is added some expression adapted to the custom. A little money to drink concludes.' In the 1970s, this custom was considered too good to lose, and was revived in Duleek. The lime is one of the largest in Ireland at 6.5m girth, and is especially fine in July when its flowering attracts bees from far and wide. You might even be tempted to bump your rump when nobody's watching, and be ready to pay for drink if caught.

The 'Freedom of Duleek' can be gained by bumping your rump against the trunk of the lime tree on the village green in Duleek

Florence Court Lime

Florence Court, Enniskillen, County Fermanagh
Tilia x *europaea* | **Lime**

HEIGHT: 21m
GIRTH: 10.96m
ACCESS: Public during advertised opening hours.

Florence Court is a large wooded estate with a magnificent Palladian house built in 1750 for John Cole MP, who named it after his mother. Two wings were added in the 1770s by his son William, who later became the first Earl of Enniskillen. It is situated a few miles west of Enniskillen at the foot of Cuilcagh Mountain, where the limestone is deeply pocked by caves along with cliffs that provide refuge for small ancient yews. The parkland is laid out in the naturalistic Romantic style of the 18th century, with grazing cattle among huge specimen trees surrounded by sheltering broadleaf woods and a scattering of silver firs, which, along with the cedar, were the largest conifers then known. In the 1840s a seven-acre pleasure ground was added close to the house, where newly discovered trees and shrubs from Asia and the west coast of America were planted. The highlight here is a weeping beech overhanging the stream. The estate was taken over by the National Trust in 1953, and opened to the public. In 1955 an accidental fire gutted the central block of the house, which has since been restored.

Park near the main entrance and take the path to Cottage Wood to visit the famous Florence Court yew. Keep an eye out for a gigantic common lime tree on your right in the parkland. It is not particularly tall at 21m, but its girth is enormous, and at just under 11m is the greatest for any broadleaf tree in Ireland. Its champion status is disputed because it is probably a bundle planting of several trees, which have fused together in the intervening 250 years. Its convoluted trunk makes it difficult to determine if it originated from a single tree that may have been damaged by grazing, coppicing or naturally sprouting new stems that then merged together. It may have been a deliberate attempt to create an instant wide-spreading tree as a landscape feature, or have come about for a reason as mundane as a worker slipping the bundle of saplings in one hole so that he could be home in time for his supper. It is now a classic and vast parkland tree, with its undercarriage kept neat and trim by ruminating cattle who appreciate its shelter.

The Florence Court lime has an enormous girth of almost 11m

Elms at Donegal Town

Lifford Road, Donegal, County Donegal
Ulmus x hollandica | **Hybrid Dutch Elm**

HEIGHT:	27m	**HEIGHT:**	27m
GIRTH:	4.7m	**GIRTH:**	4.5m
ACCESS:	These trees are located in a public graveyard and at the entrance to Donegal Town Football Club.		

A five-minute walk out along the Lifford Road from the Diamond in Donegal town will take you to the Famine graveyard overlooking the Eske River. You know you have arrived by the presence of two large elm trees inside the enclosed walls, and a beech just outside. An inscription on a memorial stone reads, 'In loving memory of those who died of hunger and disease in the Great Famine 1845–48 and were buried in the cemetery.' The workhouse was next door and these paupers were buried in the mass grave without any visible record of who they were. The larger of the elms at almost 4.5m in girth also happens to be one of the largest surviving elms in the country, and must have been planted at least 120 years ago. Or was it? Closer inspection shows it is not our native wych elm but may be a hybrid Dutch elm; it is hard to be certain as a number of elm species and hybrids were introduced from Britain and Europe in the 18th and 19th centuries. What these elms have in common is that their seed is not viable: they spread by root suckers and they may have moved into the graveyard from the adjoining hedgerow. This act of propagation also hastened their demise when Dutch elm disease rampaged through Ireland in the 1960s and 1970s, because these trees were clonal and their lack of genetic diversity meant they had little resistance to the fungal infection carried by an imported beetle. The native wych elm has viable seed, and does not sucker, so its isolation from other trees has slowed the disease's progress through our native population. County Donegal is the last stronghold of mature elm trees; lower summer temperature may be a limiting factor as it results in a low number of beetle life cycles in any one season.

Down the slope from the graveyard beside the River Eske and close to Donegal Town Football Club grounds are several more large hybrid Dutch elms. One of them, at almost 5m in girth, is the largest-known surviving elm in Ireland. They are particularly impressive in their orange tints in the late autumn sunshine. Visit them now before they inevitably succumb to disease.

Hybrid elm tree in
Donegal town

Grey Poplar in Birr

Birr Castle Demesne, Birr, County Offaly
Populus x *canescens* | **Grey Poplar**

HEIGHT:	42m
GIRTH:	6.28m
ACCESS:	The tree is located on private property but is open for public access during advertised opening hours. Admission charge. For more information visit website: www.birrcastle.ie

Birr Castle demesne is one of the greatest gardens in Ireland, with an unrivalled collection of trees from around the world. In the heart of the midlands, it lives up to its name as one the coldest places in winter, so that what survives here should grow anywhere else in Ireland. That is useful to know when considering planting in one's own garden. The 104 hectares are a combination of walled garden, woodlands and landscaped parkland on the floodplain of the River Camcor upstream of the Brosna. The 'leviathan', Birr Castle's Great Telescope, was the world's largest when it was built in the 19th century, and this huge construction, fully restored, dominates the open parkland.

The planting of exotic trees began in earnest when the fifth Earl of Rosse took over in 1908. Many of those trees, which today are champions, he planted from introductions of the great plant collector Ernest Wilson who, in the early 20th century, made the greatest number of new discoveries over four journeys to China. He died in action in the Great War. The sixth Earl continued his work, and became a great gardener in his own right, filling the gardens with introductions by other great collectors such as Augustine Henry, George Forrest and Francis Kingdon-Ward. He even went on expeditions himself to China.

With all these amazing and handsome trees, it might surprise you that the star of the gardens is a European grey poplar. Best seen from the bridge, it stands proudly beside the river, 42m tall, with a clean cylindrical stem rising high into the domed crown. The grey poplar is considered to be a natural hybrid of our native aspen and the white poplar found in continental Europe and Asia. Here is an example of two smallish trees getting together and creating a monster far outgrowing its parents. It represents the triumph of hybrid vigour. It was planted about 200 years ago, and is obviously happy on the limestone floodplain of the midlands. I found another grey poplar almost as big recently in Ferbane, County Offaly. I hope the present Lord Rosse is pleased that his signature tree remains the largest of its kind in these islands.

The largest grey poplar in both Ireland and Britain at Birr Castle

Killballyowen Horse Chestnut

Kilballyowen House, Bruff, County Limerick
Aesculus hippocastanum | **Horse Chestnut**

HEIGHT: 25m
GIRTH: 6.65m
ACCESS: The tree is located on private property. Viewing is by prior appointment only.

I got a message about five years ago telling me that there was a fine chestnut tree at an old estate near Bruff, County Limerick. Bruff only ever came on my radar during rugby internationals when that solid lump of timber John (the Bull) Hayes single-handedly kept the English maul at bay. I should have known that trees from the same place would come in similar proportions, but nothing prepared me for this tree. As I came to a fork in the drive there appeared a stupendous horse chestnut, the likes of which exist only in dreams. I can only compare it to one of the fabled banyan trees in India. Its trunk is just 6.7m in girth, and gets broader as it gets higher, before eventually dividing into a dozen huge branches that then bend over and droop to the ground. There they rest, spreading out. A couple of trunks reluctantly continue up to form a crown topping out at 25m. It wants to become a woodland, rather than a mere tree. Just imagine all this enhanced by thousands of 30cm-high panicles of flowers in early May. As soon as one of those flowers has been pollinated, the yellow base of the upper petal turns to crimson thereby signalling to bees that their service is no longer required. Then in autumn the tree provides fine fat conkers to tempt children away from their hi-tech toys. No tree could try harder to be accepted as a native but it was discovered only 400 years ago in a small area of the Balkans where Greece, Albania and Macedonia meet.

Coming from those southern mountains, it has no difficulty coping with our cool damp climate, and big trees are found just about anywhere in Ireland. It is always the first tree into leaf, and the five to seven leaflets can turn a lovely orange in autumn. This horse chestnut is not just the Irish champion: there is only one other in Europe known to be bigger. They are surprisingly long-lived, given that the timber is soft; this tree may be at least 250 years old, and could potentially live another hundred years or more, if it avoids bleeding canker and leaf miner, which are presently afflicting many of our horse chestnut trees.

Ireland's largest horse chestnut tree at Kilballyowen House

Dún a' Rí Chestnut

Dún a' Rí Forest Park, Kingscourt, County Cavan
Aesculus hippocastanum | **Horse Chestnut**

Height:	18m
Girth:	4.75m
Access:	The tree is located on property owned by Coillte and is open for public access in accordance with the company's open-forest policy.

'Fort of the King' is the English for Dún a' Rí, which suggests a long regal history for this area, while legend has Ulster's superhero Cúchulainn camping here on his way to do battle against Queen Maeve's army. This was O'Reilly territory until Cromwell came through here in 1650, inflicting defeat and confiscating the land. The next 300 years saw the Pratt family in control and consolidating their estate on the banks of the Cabra River. The old Cabra Castle was abandoned, and the Pratts moved across the road to a new mansion in the 1830s. A village with flax and corn mills serving the estate was developed on the present location of Kingscourt in 1750. The remaining 242 hectares were sold in 1959 to the state, and are now managed by Coillte as a commercial forest park. The park has a number of attractions with archaeological remains, holy wells, duck pond, river glen and trails through conifer and broadleaf woodlands. Many interesting species such as rare maples and wingnuts have been planted, enhancing the broad vistas through the park and woodland.

Our featured tree is an old horse chestnut on the edge of open parkland, before it slopes down to the river. Horse chestnuts are not related to the true edible chestnut, and their nuts are not particularly palatable to horses. They are by far the best known and most striking of large flowering trees. The Dún a' Rí chestnut is very popular with children as its layered branches provide great fun for climbing and swinging. The tree has suffered from this pastime, and has had many branches removed, which has lessened its visual impact.

Beyond the river past the Dún a' Rí chestnut is a wishing well that was probably a holy well in the distant past. The tree and well gain their fame through the popular song 'Doonaree' composed by Eilish Boland, and performed by Vera Lynn and Ruby Murray in the 1950s.

> To take the road from Dublin town way down to Doonaree,
> 'Tis there you'll find a wishing well beyond a chestnut tree,
> In a shady nook, by a winding brook,
> Will you make a wish for me.

The chestnut at Dún a' Rí Forest Park is immortalised in song

The sycamore at Gormanston College is
the most magnificent of its kind in Ireland

Gormanston Sycamore

Gormanston College, Gormanston, County Meath
Acer pseudoplatanus | **Sycamore**

HEIGHT: 25m
GIRTH: 8.33m
ACCESS: The tree is located on private property. Viewing is by prior appointment only.

If you visit only one tree in this book, then this sycamore is the one to consider. On seeing it for the first time, I was rooted to the spot in awe and admiration. It was only after going around it several times in disbelief that I had the courage to measure it, and confirm that this is perhaps the most remarkable tree in Ireland. The squashed fluted trunk is 8.3m in girth, and supports numerous branches pushing out like the spokes of a wheel, which then turn up like an umbrella blown inside-out by a strong gust of wind. Every limb seems to be straining its sinews to support the enormous domed crown 25m in the air. The best view of all is for the young and athletic, who can scramble up its central trunk which has died, leaving a stump to sit on. From there the interior is a circle of bare columns, just waiting to hide a gang of schoolchildren.

The tree may be seen near the back gate of Gormanston College on the border between County Meath and County Dublin. It is a private, fee-paying co-educational secondary school run by the Franciscans, and has been here since the 1950s when they bought Gormanston Castle and Estate. Before then it was in the possession of the Preston family, who have been Viscounts Gormanston since the 14th century.

The sycamore has increased in girth by 0.5m in the last ten years, and may be a lot younger than the 300 years I first estimated. The strain of holding up that crown is beginning to tell. Sycamores are remarkably wind-firm but if one large limb should go, this tree could fall apart like a house of cards. Conservationists and gardeners curse the sycamore's invasive offspring with great passion. A visit to this tree may be a life-changing experience. You have been warned!

SACRED TREES

Ireland hosts more sacred trees than any other country in
Europe. Sacred or protected trees go back to pre-Christian times,
when they were considered, along with other natural features
such as rocks, springs and rivers, as deities or spirits in their own
right. Trees represented a link between heaven, earth and the under-
world, and were also a home for the fairy folk or little people. Ash
and hawthorn are the most popular sacred species, while yew, oak and
crab apple also feature. Rag trees – trees festooned with pieces of cloth
representing wishes and prayers, or belonging to the person seeking the
cure – are usually hawthorn but there is a Sitka spruce at a holy well
in Kildare that has served as a rag tree since a neighbouring thorn tree
died. The Early Christian saints wisely occupied existing pagan sites,
building churches and sanctifying holy wells and their attendant rag
trees. Thousands of lone trees scattered throughout the country in
fields and ring forts also survive because they are traditionally
respected, and it is still believed that to interfere with them
might bring misfortune. My greatest wish is that all trees be
given the same respect.

St Kieran's Bush

Clareen, County Offaly
Crataegus monogyna | **Hawthorn**

HEIGHT: 4m
GIRTH: 0.57m
ACCESS: This tree can be viewed alongside the R421 public road.

Numerous fairy thorns and rag trees continue to exist in the Irish landscape. The old belief that to interfere with them will bring bad luck persists to this day. Rag trees are usually associated with holy wells. These are venerated and many are connected with fifth- and sixth-century saints. It is likely that they existed before Christianity and were sites of pagan reverence. One of the best-known rag trees can be seen by the road near Clareen, under the slopes of the Slieve Bloom Mountains. In the fifth century St Kieran was given a bell by St Patrick. He was instructed that when the bell pealed, that was the site for Kieran's monastery. St Kieran's Bush marks that spot, and nearby you can find a holy well, round tower and the remains of an Augustinian priory.

St Kieran's Bush is a relatively young hawthorn bush, which is believed to regenerate itself. When it dies, a younger bush grows up to replace it. Many years ago it was under threat of removal by the County Council during a road-widening scheme. Local people objected, and it is now preserved on an island of grass, with the old road to its west, and the new road to the east. Tradition holds that you should pass to the left of it. In the 19th century Bishop Moran of Ossory decided to show what he thought of this superstition by passing to its right. He had barely left the parish, when the shafts of his coach collapsed. You don't mess with an angry saint.

Another story tells of a man who wished to remove the bush. His co-workers refused to help unless he struck the first blow. He did, and sure enough, he suffered paralysis and died shortly afterwards. The pattern day of St Kieran is 5 March, when local people celebrate Mass and visit the holy well, graveyard and the bush. Pieces of cloth are tied to the bush, and prayers said for St Kieran's intercession and cure. Prayers are answered when the rags have rotted away.

St Kieran's bush festooned with offerings near Clareen

A lone fairy tree stands on the Hill of Tara

Fairy Tree at Tara

Hill of Tara, Navan, County Meath
Crataegus monogyna | **Hawthorn**

HEIGHT:	4m
GIRTH:	1.41m
ACCESS:	Public during advertised opening hours.

The Hill of Tara is the ancient spiritual and political capital of Ireland. Rising above the Boyne Valley, it has commanding views over a broad sweep of our island. It has ancient monuments aligned with the sun for marking the pagan festivals of Samhain in November and Imbolc in February. The Tuatha De Danann, who pre-date the Celts, used the site as their capital, and the Celts continued it as an inauguration place for the High Kings of Ireland.

At first glance there is not a lot to be seen above ground, and we would need archaeologists and historians to make sense of the grassy bumps and hollows that lie before us. There is a single hawthorn on a slope, which, like many others throughout Ireland, is known as a fairy tree. I have featured this one because it is a very beautiful and much-visited tree.

When the Celts arrived in Ireland about 300 BC the resident race known as the Tuatha De Danann were defeated, and were forced to the otherworld and became the little people or fairy folk. Every Samhain or Halloween the doors between these two worlds opened up, and the bold fairies returned to play tricks on people, hence the custom of 'trick or treat'. There is a story of an evil fairy that came to Tara every Halloween, and lulled the King and all his soldiers to sleep with his fairy music. He then burnt down the Royal Palace with fire from his mouth.

As you can see it is best not to mess with the little people, as they carry a big chip on their shoulders. Many people leave gifts and ribbons to placate them, and hope some of the magic rubs off on them. The little people reside at lone trees, raths and other sacred places, and that is why such places are generally left alone, for fear of misfortune. Why take chances?

Fairy Thorn at Rubble

Rubble, Killasser, Swinford, County Mayo
Crataegus monogyna | **Hawthorn**

HEIGHT: 5m

GIRTH: 1.35m

ACCESS: This tree is inaccessible but can be seen from the L1329 or Killasser road off the N26, 3 km north-west of Swinford.

Killasser in east Mayo lies in the lee of the Ox Mountains, in the valley of the Moy River near Swinford. The land consists of rich limestone pastures, with several lakes fed by the high rainfall running off the mountains. People have lived here for thousands of years, and have left numerous archaeological remains undisturbed to the present. An ancient ring fort at Rubble features one of the most dramatic fairy thorns in the country. Our ancestors certainly could teach estate agents a thing or two with the refrain 'location, location, location!'

The ring fort commands views for miles around, and is in close proximity to the finest salmon fishery in the land. The ring fort is a very impressive grassy mound capped by a twin-stemmed hawthorn, when seen from the road below. Getting up to it is tricky, with hedges and squelchy streams to negotiate.

Once there, you can appreciate the hawthorn's impact and presence, which is heightened by its regal appearance and perfection. It is huge for a hawthorn in such an exposed place. It has been respected by man and beast for at least 200 years and left in quiet isolation to the little folk. A couple of fields away lies another rath or ring fort called 'Black Patch', surrounded by a circle of hawthorns with a few scattered rocks. It is a *cillín* or burial place for unbaptised children. Canon Law dictated that unbaptised or still-born children could not be interred in consecrated ground. The burial in such a place probably reflects the subliminal belief in its sanctity and connection with the other world, passed down through the ages, which helped protect lone or fairy trees. Let us hope that all such trees and places remain undisturbed.

A lone hawthorn atop one of the many ancient ring forts near Killasser in east Mayo

St Flannan's Well, Inagh

Inagh, County Clare
Fraxinus excelsior | **Ash**

HEIGHT: 14m
GIRTH: 2.55m
ACCESS: The access path is fenced off from adjoining private property to enable public access from the road to the well. The well is located at grid reference 122293.167/184451.695.

Over 3,000 holy wells are thought to exist in Ireland. Many are believed to have originated before Christianity, and their divinity was borrowed and transferred to the early saints, after whom many were named. It made a lot of sense to overlay pagan sacred places with the new beliefs, and carry the people with you. Wells express a folk approach to the divine, whether people are seeking a spiritual cleansing, or a cure, and many old traditions associated with wells have survived to modern times. Trees at wells are an important element as a repository for coins, pins, rags and religious iconography.

One of the most popular wells, and my personal favourite, with a wonderful tree, is found in the centre of County Clare at Inagh. In the seventh century St Flannan from east Clare, the first Bishop of Killaloe, did a fierce amount of travelling, and ended up at a sacred grove here in Inagh, where he took a rest, leaving his footprints on a stone and his blessing on the well. How he found it I do not know, as I got lost and did several U-turns before stumbling on the long path around several fields which eventually stops at the edge of the woodland.

You become aware that this is a captivating place when you see fresh flowers in jam jars, and blue-painted washing machines hosting religious pictures, with a hubcap hanging from a tree, followed by white-painted stones. Could St Flannan be the patron saint of recycling? This atmospheric sanctuary is crowned by an old ash tree in the middle, with massive angular branches festooned with ferns and moss. Attached to the trunk is a plastic barrel hosting more religious pictures. At its base is a coffin-shaped collection of stones, where you can do penance by lying down. The tree is called the 'unusual tree' for no apparent reason; it just is. This sacred sanctuary is looked after with love and care, and its pattern day falls on 18 December, when pilgrims do the rounds. You have to visit it to witness how magic and tradition still exist today.

The ash tree at the popular
St Flannan's Well at Inagh

St Bernard's Well, Rathkeale

Rathkeale, County Limerick
Fraxinus excelsior | **Ash**

HEIGHT: 12m
GIRTH: 3.77m
ACCESS: This tree is located on private property which is open to public access.

It was not difficult to get directions to St Bernard's Well from devotees at the Holy Stump at St Mary's Church in Rathkeale. The Holy Stump in the image of the Virgin Mary became headline news in recent times, when thousands of pilgrims flocked to pay homage. A few miles outside Rathkeale on a narrow country road, a fingerpost lets you know that you have arrived. The roofless church of St Beinid stands alone as a reminder of the destruction of Catholic churches in the 16th and 17th centuries. Beyond it is St Beinid or St Bernard's Well, which in reality is a broad pond fed by spring water bubbling to the surface, with a mighty ash tree protecting it. There are a couple of other ash trees to keep it company, and to take over its role of repository of relics, rags and other offerings, if the big old ash should ever succumb.

The tree has a huge branch erupting from the base and spreading like an upturned hand over the well. It must be one of the most peaceful and atmospheric holy well sites in the country, and is well visited and looked after. Such sites have been places of devotion for millennia, and became more important during penal times when the official Church was outlawed. The traditional date for the feast of St Bernard is 20 August, when pilgrims would do the rounds, say prayers and drink the water, which was reputed to cure lameness, rheumatism and sore eyes. Offerings such as coins were left in the well, and rags tied to the tree.

The well gradually fell into disuse a hundred years ago, as it became the haunt of farm animals. A local committee was set up and the site was restored in 1980 with railings and steps put in by the tree to the well. Large crowds have returned, especially on Good Friday and St Bernard's feast day. The well has never dried up, which is good for the legendary trout, which if spotted will cure all ailments.

St Bernard's Well near Rathkeale is overhung by an immense ash tree

Protectively wrapped around St Benin's Well near Tuam are the enormous roots of an ash tree

St Benin's Well, Kilbannon

Kilbannon, Tuam, County Galway
Fraxinus excelsior | **Ash**

HEIGHT:	13m
GIRTH:	4.92m
ACCESS:	This tree is located on private property off the R332 road between Tuam and Ballinrobe at Kilbannon.

Two miles outside Tuam on the Ballinrobe road is Kilbannon Church with its round tower, where St Benin founded a monastery back in the fifth century. St Patrick passed through here on his way to Croagh Patrick where is it reputed that he baptised the Celts in the waters of the well. As a boy St Benin was present when St Patrick preached, and he became so attached to the preacher that nothing could separate them. Eventually St Patrick appointed Benin to head the church and monastery at Kilbannon, and later St Benin succeeded St Patrick as Bishop of Armagh. No trace of the early foundation remains. The round tower was built in about AD 1000, and the annals record the burning of the site in 1114. The Franciscans came here in 1428, and built the church, now in ruins, and the site subsequently became a graveyard for the local community.

Beyond the graveyard, in a field, you will find one of the most remarkable trees in Ireland. It is an old ash tree which is wrapping itself around St Benin's Well and resembles a Hindu mystic meditating in the lotus position. Perhaps it is just tired after standing up to 250 years of storms, and is resting on its haunches. The outer ring of hawthorns does not ease its burden, but at least their blossoms in May must raise its spirit. Between the tree and the well is an enclosing wall which keeps livestock at bay. Unfortunately the Corrib drainage scheme dropped the water table in the 1950s so that the well is now dry except during wet winters. In the early 20th century a local priest put a stop to the shenanigans which occurred during the annual Garland Sunday on the last Sunday of July. Prayers were repeated and the faithful would walk around the well seven times. Coins were thrown in, and religious objects placed around the well, and afterwards the festivities began to which the priest took exception. The tree still welcomes courting couples to its embrace without any moral judgement.

Ash at St Patrick's Well, Dromard

Dromard, County Sligo
Fraxinus excelsior | **Ash**

HEIGHT: 14m
GIRTH: 3.15m
ACCESS: The tree is located on private property. Viewing is by prior appointment only.

The veneration of wells and trees is an ancient and widespread tradition, going back to pre-Christian times. The country took some time to be converted, and pagan practices were given a veneer of Christianity, while deities were replaced by the early Irish saints. A belief in the sacred and healing powers of wells and trees continues up to the present day, and St Patrick's Well at Dromard is a prime example. Dromard is on the road between Sligo and Ballina with splendid views of Sligo Bay, Knocknarea and Benbulben in the distance. St Patrick's Well is a short drive along country boreens at the foot of the Ox Mountains. It is reputed to be the oldest well in Connaught, and to have been consecrated by St Patrick himself. He found it necessary to baptise his converts at wayside wells and springs which were already sacred. Mass and devotions are held at the well on the feast day of Saints Peter and Paul which is 29 June. Turas or rounds are performed by penitents in a clockwise direction in their bare feet. This involves prayers, the sipping of water and the washing of feet.

There are two fine ash trees within the enclosed walls of the well, and there used to be a bigger and older tree which had a hollow filled with water. It is said that hawkers started to sell the water and that a priest had it cut down but then the water miraculously reappeared in the fork of one of the present trees on the feast day. Bark from the trees also had the power to cure backache and devotees carried pieces on their person for relief. It is remarkable and life-affirming that these ancient customs and beliefs still continue into the 21st century.

An ash tree overlooks the sacred site
of St Patrick's Well at Dromard

St Fintan's Money Tree

Clonenagh, Mountrath, County Laois
Acer pseudoplatanus | **Sycamore**

HEIGHT: 5m
GIRTH: 0.57m
ACCESS: Public. The tree is located alongside the R445 between Portlaoise and Mountrath.

Beside the old Limerick road between Portlaoise and Mountrath are the remains of an old monastery dedicated to the sixth-century St Fintan, who was born in the locality. Not far away in a field was a holy well also dedicated to St Fintan, which attracted many devotees. Back in the 19th century, the landowner, tired of the troublesome and superstitious visitors, had the well closed over. Soon after water was seen to have risen up in a large sycamore tree beside the monastery, and formed a miraculous pool high in the crown. It was a sign of St Fintan's displeasure at the well's desecration. The tree became the focus of devotion, and people climbed up the trunk to make a wish and tie a rag for good luck. As time went by coins were hammered into the trunk, and soon every branch was covered with metal, which must have undermined the tree's health. There are many instances of other tree wells around the country, and none seem to have survived, as eventually water sitting in a fork or cavity will rot the tree. The tree fell in a storm in 1994 leaving a dead stump and pieces of coin-encrusted timber for souvenir hunters to scavenge. That should have been the end of the story, but perhaps miracles do still happen as the stump has re-sprouted and now has several stems rising to 4.5m. Maybe it should be called the immortal tree.

New life has emerged from the stump of the renowned St Fintan's money tree near Mountrath

LANDMARK & JUNCTION TREES

Landmark trees speak for themselves. Look at me, am I not great?! They may not be that big, but can take advantage of crowning the highest point around, their leaves proudly billowing like a strutting peacock. This exposure has a cost, of course, as they bear the brunt of what storms throw at them, but the constant buffeting forces the roots to dig deep with an extra-firm grip. They tend to attract one's gaze, giving a focal point in the landscape and completing the picture of the artist's or photographer's composition. Junction trees are scattered thinly throughout the country, with the most surviving in rural Leinster. They come in all shapes and sizes, and are under constant threat from road widening and traffic collisions. Some may stand on a small green, while others look stressed surrounded by tarmac. Many have beautifully constructed retaining walls protecting the trunk, or a seat placed under them, thereby turning them into meeting places and adding greatly to our landscape heritage.

Hawthorn on Freestone Hill

Freestone Hill, Coolgrange, Cliften, County Kilkenny
Crataegus monogyna | **Hawthorn**

HEIGHT: 3m
GIRTH: 0.65m
ACCESS: The tree is located on private property. Viewing is by prior appointment only. It is visible from the R702, old Kilkenny to Gowran Road.

Approaching Kilkenny city on the old Carlow road, one's gaze can't help but be drawn up to Freestone Hill, an outlying flank of the Castlecomer plateau. Weaving hedgerows climb up and eventually stop short of the summit, capped by a lonely hawthorn. Look carefully and you will see that the remains of a ring fort encircle the summit, and a small cement trig point of the Ordnance Survey keeps the bush company. It is the very epitome of a fairy tree and meeting place of the little people, who have lived on in folk memory since pagan times.

Arriving at the summit, the stupendous view of the Barrow Valley, with a backdrop of the Wicklow and Blackstairs Mountains, makes you realise that this is a significant site of command and control. Archaeologists have discovered burnt bodies buried here, along with Roman bronze pieces, jewellery and coins from the fourth century, which may have been pagan votive offerings. Evidence was also uncovered of the earliest known ore extraction from the Bronze Age in Ireland.

Alas, when you approach the tree you can see that someone attempted to cut it down about twenty years ago, leaving just one stem intact, propped up as a saw failed to cut through it. Apparently three local lads were to blame, and tempted the fate that many believe would bring them harm. A lifetime exposed to the elements has toughened the hawthorn tree against the elements, and it shows the windswept form usually associated with hawthorns on Atlantic shores. It could be very old, and a replacement for a previous hawthorn. Beware about going there with a lass from the local parish of Clara, for it is said that there is then no chance of escaping marriage with her.

The lone hawthorn tree on the summit of Freestone Hill is a well-known landmark in Kilkenny

The tree's windswept appearance has been moulded by its exposed hilltop location

Clipped Hawthorn

Ballymount, Calverstown, County Kildare
Crataegus monogyna | **Hawthorn**

HEIGHT: 3m
GIRTH: 0.9m
ACCESS: Public. The tree is located alongside the R448 between Timolin and Kilcullen.

Beside the old Dublin road between Timolin and Kilcullen stands a hawthorn clipped into the shape of a cross. Since childhood I had been curious about the reason for it, and it always pleased me to see it maintained every year. Here is its story and how it came about: it was the evening of the All-Ireland hurling final in September 1933 when Matt Doyle walked the road near Ballymount Church on his way to buy cigarettes at the local shop. Traffic was heavy with the returning Kilkenny supporters after another glorious victory. Matt was dazzled by the oncoming headlights and was struck by a Model T Ford and died in hospital from his injuries a few days later. Matt was a very popular figure in the area, and two neighbours tied a hawthorn bush into the shape of a cross at the accident spot. It was a commemorative gesture, and what is surprising is that the bush is maintained to this day. Two of his grandsons visit and clip the bush every 10 September, on Matt's anniversary. In centuries past, this tradition was common at an accident site and today there are many stone memorials to victims of traffic accidents but this is the only living cross that I know of. It is appropriate that a hawthorn was chosen, as they are associated with holy wells and fairy raths and thus less likely to be harmed for fear of retribution.

Planting a tree or clipping a hawthorn is, I think, the most fitting memorial, as life is more beautiful than death.

This clipped hawthorn at Ballymount in Kildare is a distinctive roadside memorial to a local man

Dancing Tree of Cloncurry

Enfield, County Meath
Fraxinus excelsior | **Ash**

HEIGHT: 19m
GIRTH: 4.08m
ACCESS: The tree is located on private property but is visible from the adjoining Cloncurry cemetery.

Dancing trees may be trees or bushes that in times past marked a place in rural areas, often a crossroads, where dances and other social events took place. Such meeting places no longer exist but 'Dancing Trees' that sway and dance in the breeze on mounds and summits are found throughout the midlands.

One tree that fits this description is an old ash crowning a motte beside Cloncurry graveyard and church near Enfield, just over the Kildare boundary beside the old Dublin road. Locally called the Dancing Tree, it must be quite old for in 1875, Canon O'Hanlon, a Catholic priest who compiled many works of historical and religious significance wrote, 'A remarkable moat or aboriginal earthwork adjoins the cemetery and on its summit rises a well-grown tree, which presents a very picturesque object from all approaches.' The motte is in a private farmer's field and a scramble up its slope will make you appreciate its steep defensive qualities even without its former timber palisade.

Motte and baileys were forts built by the Anglo-Normans soon after their invasion in the 12th century. They were replaced by stone castles, and eventually by the 15th century, the Norman colonists were integrated with the native Irish to such an extent that English control receded to an area around Dublin called the Pale. The motte at Cloncurry was then given a new lease of life as part of the ditches and ramparts constructed to defend the Pale from the raiding Irish. The medieval village of Cloncurry disappeared after ending up on the wrong side of the Pale.

About 15km away, at Clonard in County Meath, stands another motte by the road on the Hill of Doon. On its summit stands a dancing tree planted in the 19th century, only this time it is a billowing lime, which must hum with the sound of insects hunting nectar in summer.

So what makes a tree a dancing tree? Movement and grace in a breeze would be a requisite, and for me it must appear to have climbed to the highest point around, with the imaginary intention of taking flight.

A 'dancing' ash tree crowns a motte beside Cloncurry graveyard near Enfield

In the distant view stands a 'dancing' beech on top of
an ancient burial mound at Rahugh near Kilbeggan

An ancient hawthorn tree with stems
interwoven into a twist at Rahugh

Dancing Beech and Twisted Thorn at Rahugh

Rahugh, Kilbeggan, County Westmeath
Fagus sylvatica | **Beech**

HEIGHT: 14m
GIRTH: 2.69m
ACCESS: This tree is located on privately owned land but is visible from Tinnycross Road.

Rahugh lies by an esker ridge a few kilometres north of Tullamore on the boundary between Westmeath and Offaly. Eskers were formed within ice-walled tunnels fed by streams and rivers that flowed within and under glaciers during the ice age. When the ice melted it left long winding ridges of sand and gravel, often several kilometres long, above the midland plains. The greatest esker (in fact a collection of conjoined eskers) runs from Galway to Dublin dividing Ireland into two halves. This collection of eskers is known as Esker Riada, and provided a route to travel above the bogs in ancient times. In those days it was called '*an tSlí Mhór*', meaning The Great Way, and was one of five great highways that led to Tara.

Straddling Esker Riada at Rahugh is a barrow or prehistoric burial mound, standing among grassy slopes with magnificent views over the pastoral landscape of the midlands. Crowning the barrow is a beech tree, perfectly symmetrical and poised between heaven and earth. It is not particularly old or big, but its presence draws one's gaze from wherever you view it.

This awe-inspiring place may be a little off the beaten track now but during the ninth century it was used as a place of assembly where kings held peace talks. Later it was used as an inauguration site for local chieftains, and a processional way led down to the monastery and church of Rahugh. Close to the T-junction is a fingerpost to the church in a private farmer's field. Rahugh is an early Christian church founded on the site of a rath by St Hugh, who was a great-great grandson of the legendary Niall of the Nine Hostages.

The path to the church follows an old track with several ancient-looking hawthorns of great size and presence. One of them has got itself in a knot with three trunks of equal size interweaving as if to pool their strength and challenge any buffeting that storms might throw at it. Thorns have long been associated with crown of thorns Christ suffered to wear on the cross and a traditional chant to prevent pricks from festering is:

> Christ was of a virgin born, And he was pricked with a thorn,
> And it did neither bell nor swell, And I trust in Jesus this never will.

Today, people visit the headache stone at the church for a cure. The story goes that when St Hugh's mother gave birth to him after a long hard labour, he fell with such force that his head left a hollow on the stone she sat on. Headaches are cured by resting one's head in the hollow.

Foulkesmill's Junction Tree

Foulkesmill, County Wexford
Quercus petraea | **Sessile Oak**

HEIGHT: 9m
GIRTH: 3.42m
ACCESS: Public

Junction trees are a reminder of a gentler, less hectic past. They seem to say no to our headlong rush to get through our villages and countryside as quickly as possible. They are focal points, which can provide shade, shelter and perhaps even a seat. I have recorded many from Tipperary through Leinster into Ulster. They survive by the efforts of local communities, and enlightened county councils.

One of the best examples can be seen in the pretty village of Foulkesmill in south County Wexford. It is a sessile oak, which is usually associated with the acidic soils of our hills, but seems perfectly happy surrounded by tarmac. The tree once formed the corner of a garden, which was acquired by the council to facilitate increased traffic. They widened the T-junction, and provided another lane so that the oak would be left in the middle as a signature tree. A lovely circular retaining wall was built to protect the trunk. Extensive tree surgery was carried out a few years ago to reduce the crown. It was paid for by the Tidy Towns Committee despite local fear that this would damage the tree. The crown has re-grown and this is helping to extend its life.

The sessile and common oak look very similar, and one way to tell them apart is that the leaf of the sessile oak is wedge-shaped at its base on a longer leaf stalk than the common oak, whose leaf stalks are almost hidden by basal lobes.

Maybe we should try and persuade our county councils to plant a signature tree in the middle of our roundabouts, and take a leaf from the past?

The junction tree in
Foulkesmill, County Wexford

Streamstown Junction Tree

Streamstown, County Westmeath
Fagus sylvatica | **Common Beech**

HEIGHT:	22m
GIRTH:	3.81m
ACCESS:	Public

Back in 2003 Streamstown gained notoriety for coming last in Ireland in the Tidy Towns competition. It was not the first nor even the last time it gained that dubious honour. It was described in newspapers as on a road not going to or from anywhere. It was a sorry sight of dilapidated buildings, big ugly signs, and a pub at the crossroads, called The Beech Tree, badly in need of a lick of paint. The beech tree across the road was portrayed as ancient and gnarled, standing in all its magnificence among the detritus of discarded fast-food cartons, cans and plastic bottles. A local farmer was quoted as saying 'What difference does it make to a place like this whether its tidy or not?' I knew nothing of this when I slammed on my brakes at the crossroads during a wet summer's evening in 2009. Before me stood a glorious junction beech tree, on a bed of gravel in front of a stone wall, with a delightful Gothic metal seat around the trunk. Its wet grey trunk rose like a column into the crown 22m up. It seemed to be declaring that this is somewhere, and that I am proud to be here. Sometime in the intervening years the local community must have had enough of the disparaging remarks and transformed the village's appearance to that of understated beauty, and a destination in its own right. Beauty and decay are never far apart, such as the fungi and yeasts that produce the world's great wines and blue cheeses. Beech wood infected by fungi can be very valuable when turned, or made into furniture. From a national low of 127 points in 2003, by 2012 Streamstown had climbed up to 243 marks in the Tidy Towns competition.

Big Tree of Kilcurry

Kilcurry, Dundalk, County Louth
Acer pseudoplatanus | **Sycamore**

Height: 18m
Girth: 4.04m
Access: Public

The big tree at Kilcurry crossroads on the road between Dundalk and Armagh is one of the most dramatic landmark trees in the country. It demands attention from whatever direction you approach it. By their trees shall you know the people and the place. There used to be many such trees around the country, but being big has its drawbacks as it is likely to be old, and in the way of road widening. County councils and landowners are fearful of being sued in this age of litigation, and insurers do not like the risks involved in leaving large old trees in place. Utility pipes and cables are usually buried under roads, which involves trenching and cutting through roots which further endangers roadside trees. So it is a wonder this tree still stands.

The local community of Kilcurry should be congratulated on protecting and speaking on behalf of the oldest denizen in their area. A plaque by the tree states 'The big tree stands at the junction of three town lands: Carrickedmond, Balriggan and Kilcurry. It is estimated that this sycamore is now about 195 years old. It was planted by Margaret Grant, who was born in 1812, as a sapling given to her by her father. It has survived a fire, which destroyed an old hall on the other side of the road in 1977, numerous automobile collisions, and more recently, the threat of removal to facilitate road realignment in 2005.' It is also recorded that a meeting to organise the Land League in County Louth was held under the big tree in 1879. This sycamore is 18m high and 4m in girth, with a splendid wide crown sweeping over the road.

Sycamore is the largest and longest-living member of the maple family. It is from southern Europe and is the best choice as a wind break from Atlantic storms. A great regret I have is not being able to prevent the removal of a lovely sycamore at my own local crossroads during road realignment. I did not know it was under threat and suddenly it was gone. I should have been more vigilant. The Kilcurry sycamore is a landmark tree, witness tree, junction tree and big tree all rolled into one. Treasure it.

The Big Tree of Kilcurry is a large sycamore marking the junction of three local townlands

Lime tree at Kilbraghan Crossroads

Kilbraghan Lime Tree

Kilbraghan Cross Roads, Kilmanagh, County Kilkenny
Tilia x *europaea* | **Common Lime**

HEIGHT: 18m
GIRTH: 5.05m
ACCESS: Public

Among the rolling hills, high hedgerows and green pastures of west Kilkenny one may think that time has stood still. This is dairy country, where twice a day traffic jams are created by cows being herded home for milking. Near the Tipperary boundary lies the little hamlet of Kilbraghan, where five roads meet and a few houses huddle together for comfort. Back in 1875 the Rev. J. Holahan, in his *Notes on the Antiquities of the United Parishes of Ballycallan, Killmanagh and Killaloe,* describing Kilbraghan, wrote 'Five roads meet at this village, which seems to have seen better days. At the crossroads there grows a very fine, wide spreading lime tree, which is beautiful to behold in summer, and affords a most agreeable shade to the traveller.'

Those comments still apply today, as the lime stands proudly 18.2m high and 22.8m in spread, with a girth of 5m in a green space just about able to contain it. The tree must be at least 250 years of age, considering its magnificence in 1875. Signposts are few and far between for Kilbraghan, but who needs them when one has this tree to signpost your arrival? In times past it was the meeting place for the young fellows to hang out smoking and telling stories, and getting up to no good playing skittles or waiting for a lift to the hurling match. People don't hang out there any more; television and the motor car have taken care of that. It is only the occasional lost tourist who might stop in their tracks to pay respect to this living monumental landmark, and wonder which of the five roads to take next. Well, listen carefully to the murmuring of the tree, and give thanks to the person who planted it, and all those who live in its shadow for treasuring it.

John Kavanagh's Tree

Limbrick Cross Roads, Killinierin, County Wexford
Juglans regia | **Walnut**

HEIGHT: 11m
GIRTH: 1.78m
ACCESS: Public

Back in the early years of the last century John Kavanagh worked as a farmhand on the Esmonde estate. They were popular landlords, and employed as many as 18 people on their farm in north County Wexford. One day, John decided he wanted an apple tree for his front garden; he lived in the old RIC barracks at Limbrick Hill crossroads, just up the road from Killinierin. There was a young sapling growing on the estate, and John rescued it and proudly planted it.

The tree grew well for a few years without producing any apples. It slowly dawned on him that it was not an apple tree, but not knowing what it was, he had his son plant it on the grass island at the crossroads. Typically for this species, it was many years later before it fruited for the first time. It is a walnut tree, which is native to a region running from the Balkans all the way to China. They grow as well as anywhere in Ireland, but need a hot summer to fruit reliably. The timber is very valuable and is sought for making gunstocks, quality furniture and veneer. This tree, though, is under more threat from passing vehicles than timber merchants.

Mr Kavanagh may have been botanically challenged, but he showed great expertise in moving the tree twice. Walnut trees hate being transplanted and often die as a result. Oh, and there is now a real apple tree in John Kavanagh's front garden.

A walnut at Limbrick crossroads is known as John Kavanagh's tree

GREAT AVENUES & HISTORIC LANDSCAPES

An avenue is a straight road lined with trees on both sides leading to a house or landscape feature. Usually a single species is planted, and preferably a clone, such as the common lime, so that a regular form or shape is maintained. It was in France in the 17th and 18th centuries that the planting of great avenues came to a head. Great parks and gardens were laid out in geometric designs, and trees were used as mere building blocks. This fashion was soon adopted in Britain and Ireland, as estates were established and avenues created to enhance the new mansion and impress the visitor. Lime, beech and yew were the most popular trees planted at the time. In the late 18th century a natural landscape park style became the fashion, replacing stiff formality, but more often than not the main avenue continued to be planted in a straight line. New tree species were tried in the 19th century, and the following pages contain exotics which were successfully used. Also included is the J. F. Kennedy Arboretum as a modern example of integrating all these exotic discoveries into a planned landscape. Tree planting became integral to city streetscapes and many fine examples are described in this section by Dr Christy Boylan, former Senior Parks Superintendent in South County Dublin Council.

Chesterfield Avenue in Phoenix Park

Chesterfield Avenue

Phoenix Park, Dublin
Tilia platyphyllos 'Rubra' | **Red-twigged Lime and variants**
Aesculus hippocastanum and *A. hippocastanum* 'Baumanii' | **Horse Chestnut**
Fagus sylvatica | **Beech**

Avenue Length:	3.62km
Access:	Public

Chesterfield Avenue was created in Phoenix Park by the fourth Earl of Chesterfield, Lord Lieutenant of Ireland, in the mid-1740s. The original avenue was realigned and replanted in the 1840s by the architect Decimus Burton, extending for 2¼ miles (3.62km) in a straight line from the Parkgate Street entrance to Castleknock Gate. The long avenue lacks the conventional focal point at its end, but the Phoenix Monument, located approximately halfway along the route, provides an ideal alternative. The central carriageway is 12.8m wide with raised footpaths on each side separated from the road by wide grass margins. In the 1990s the original footpaths were converted to cycleways, and new footpaths built between the trees.

Decimus Burton chose to plant the avenue with English elm (*Ulmus procera*). *Tilia platyphyllos* cv 'Rubra' (Corallina), the red-twigged lime, was added after consultations with Sir William Hooker, Director of Kew Gardens, and Mr James Mackay, Curator of Trinity College Botanic Gardens. Its attractive appearance, fast growth and wind resistance influenced the choice, following severe storm damage to the park in 1839. However, the initial planting did not thrive, and the avenue was replanted in 1898 with two additional species in a unique arrangement of three rows, with trees at 18m apart. The red-twigged limes were planted again, with two specimens, one behind the other, forming two rows on each side of the road. This was interspersed with horse chestnut, and the sequence of lime, horse chestnut, lime, horse chestnut was repeated along the avenue. Behind these two rows a third row of beech was planted in positions offset from the other rows, giving three rows of trees on either side of the main road.

These trees have endured a number of storms since 1898, with the loss of some specimens. Over the years, dangerous branches have been removed and gaps replanted, ensuring that it will remain an important feature of the park for many years to come. Interestingly the replacement horse chestnut trees are *A. hippocastanum* 'Baumanii', the sterile species, which will not produce conkers that might become a hazard so near to busy footpaths, cycleways and the road.

St Anne's Park

Clontarf, Dublin 3
Quercus ilex | **Evergreen Oak**
Pinus radiata | **Monterey Pine**
Pinus nigra subsp. *nigra* | **Austrian Pine**

AVENUE LENGTH:	1.5km
ACCESS:	Public

St Anne's Park in Clontarf, now the second largest municipal park in Dublin, was formerly a private estate comprising more than 200 hectares, owned by the Guinness family. In 1873 it passed down to Lord and Lady Ardilaun who were considered to be Francophiles. They made many changes to the house and grounds including grand *allées* radiating from the house planted with *Quercus ilex,* the evergreen oak, which was a great favourite of Lord Ardilaun. He raised thousands of these trees from acorns and distributed them to others. There is a fine belt of evergreen oak in the Phoenix Park, said to have been donated by Lord Ardilaun. It has been said that most of the evergreen oaks in the Dublin region arose from acorns collected from the trees in St Anne's Park. These oak specimens are interplanted with Monterey pine (*Pinus radiata*) and Austrian pine (*Pinus nigra* subsp. *nigra).*

Even though the mansion is no longer there to serve as a focal point, the impressive avenue provides interest and shelter for the many people who use the park daily. These oak trees ripple beyond the park, and can easily be seen when travelling through Raheny on the Howth Road. As evidence of the resilience of oak trees, I can recall when the entire avenue of oak trees was infested with tortrix moth around 1990. They had significantly defoliated the trees but when the larval cycle was completed, the trees produced new growth and recovered very quickly. The infestation seems to have been a once-off, as to my knowledge the moths did not return.

The heritage of tree planting in St Anne's estate was the inspiration for the Tree Council of Ireland to undertake the development of the Millennium Arboretum in 1988 when Dublin city was celebrating its first millennium. Sponsored by the public for £25 per tree, the 6.5-hectare arboretum is located adjacent to the main avenue. It includes 1,000 different trees planted in continental groupings. Most of the trees have established well and are now very interesting specimens of their type – no doubt they will be heritage trees for future generations to record.

The main avenue in St Anne's Park planted with evergreen oak

View of internal avenue of evergreen oak adjacent to the main avenue at St Anne's Park

Lime trees define the mile-long Prince of Wales Avenue leading from the Parliament Buildings at Stormont

Lime Avenue at Stormont Castle

Belfast, County Antrim
Tilia platyphyllos 'Rubra' | **Red-twigged Lime**

AVENUE LENGTH:	0.9km
ACCESS:	Public

The site for the parliament building at Stormont was chosen in the 1920s, and the new parliament building and landscape completed by 1932. The Lime Avenue is made up of four rows of red-twigged limes totalling 305 trees, and was planted in 1928 on the advice of Mr W. J. Bean, former curator of Kew Gardens. At that time elms were considered but fortunately not chosen as they most likely would have succumbed to Dutch elm disease during the 1960s and 1970s. The trees were planted at 12m apart, with 60m between the inner rows at the lower end of the avenue increasing to 76m at the upper end. The Parliament Building appears by the illusion of fore-shortened perspective to be closer to the entrance than it is. Officially named Prince of Wales Avenue, but also known locally as the 'Mile', the avenue is actually 900m from the Newtownards Road entrance to Carson's Monument at the upper end.

Because of waterlogging the ground level was raised around the bases of some of the trees shortly after planting. This had the desired effect as all the trees survived until 1986 when two died. These were replaced with semi-mature trees which have thrived and are now about 9m tall.

Contractors have maintained the Lime Avenue since 1981 and they restrict all pruning to removal of dead or broken branches for site safety and annually carry out minor crown lifting, removing an average 30 cm of previous year's growth to give a uniform 'base' to the tree crown. This and the removal of epicormic growth maintains the neat appearance of the avenue.

This wide avenue contains several lines of lime trees which fade into a woodland at the rear. The statue of Lord Carson on the rising ground before the castle is an attractive added feature. In my view, this is the most spectacular lime avenue in Ireland. What makes this scene so great is the wonderful focal point of the castle, and the dip in the intermediate ground which magnifies the impact.

Griffith Avenue

Dublin

Platanus x *hispanica (syn. P. acerifolia)* | **London Plane**
Acer pseudoplatanus | **Sycamore**
Acer platanoides | **Norway Maple**
Fagus sylvatica | **Beech**
Aesculus hippocastanum | **Horse Chestnut**
Betula alba | **Birch**

AVENUE LENGTH:	4km
ACCESS:	Public

Griffith Avenue on Dublin's north side is even longer than Chesterfield Avenue in the Phoenix Park. It extends from Marino to Glasnevin and Drumcondra, a distance of approximately 4km. The only city street in Dublin with a double line of trees, it was created between 1924 and 1928 as Dublin's first all-concrete road. In contrast to the *Avenue des Champs-Élysées*, it does not have any retail outlets. Instead it is fronted entirely by housing, schools or churches. The wide road margins on both sides of the avenue are divided by a footpath which is one of the most pleasant pedestrian routes in the city. Perhaps because it is located on the north side of the city, it is less well known and seldom photographed but it is a very elegant and picturesque streetscape, which many use frequently commuting to and from the city.

The trees are all the same height but the species range is quite diverse. It seems that the planting policy – if such existed – was to plant in blocks, so for, say 100m, all the trees on one side are London plane (*Platanus x hispanica (syn. P. acerifolia)*). The next line would be maples or sycamores (*Acer platanoides* and *Acer pseudoplatanus*), beech (*Fagus sylvatica*) or horse chestnut (*Aesculus hippocastanum*). There are some birch (*Betula alba*) trees as well and they have grown large; their white stems add variety.

Because all the trees appear to be the same height, they make a significant impact, and the different species are not noticeable until spring when the horse chestnuts are the first to open bud, and display their attractive candle-like flowers. Likewise in autumn the maples provide a rich colour beside the plane trees, which remain green for some months more. The usual recommendation for avenue planting is to plant the same tree species. However, Griffith Avenue is an exception because of its scale, and the matching tree sizes. It is truly one of Dublin's greatest landscape features.

Tree-lined Griffith Avenue on the north side of Dublin

The road through Herbert Park in Dublin is lined with hornbeam trees

Hornbeam Avenue at Herbert Park

Ballsbridge, Dublin 4
Carpinus betulus 'Fastigiata' | **Fastigiate Hornbeam**

AVENUE LENGTH:	300m
ACCESS:	Public

Most city parks are developed along informal lines, with a range of active and passive facilities. The designers' intention is to encourage visitors to stay awhile, and that means favouring sinuous pathways rather than straight lines. An exception is Herbert Park in Dublin 4, which comprises two sections divided by a road. The park was developed after the 1907 World Trade Exhibition and opened in 1911.

The road dividing the two sections is called Herbert Park and between 1912 and 1916 various dignitaries planted specimens of Wheatley elms (*Ulmus wheatleyi*) which, in the decades that followed, were a significant landscape feature in the city. They succumbed to Dutch elm disease and were felled in 1984. A similar line of Wheatley elms alongside River Road near the banks of the Tolka River near Glasnevin also died around the same time. Elms were less popular in Ireland than in England, and the suckering ability of the English elm (*Ulmus procera syn. U. campestris*) made it more suitable for hedgerows rather than avenues. Therefore the loss of elms from disease had less impact in Ireland, except in the Limerick area where elms were more prevalent. Elm species planted since then are considered resistant to the disease.

The elms at Herbert Park were replaced in 1985 by upright hornbeams (*Carpinus betulus* 'Fastigiata'). This planting marked the first National Tree Week held by the Tree Council of Ireland. The hornbeam is one of those trees that generally fits in anywhere because of its upright habit. For street trees, it is usually 'the right tree in the right place'. Hornbeams also look well on Kylemore Road, Dublin between Long Mile Road and Walkinstown Avenue. Its infrequent planting in other areas is due mainly to a lack of availability in sufficient numbers.

Lime Avenue at Marina

Marina, Cork, County Cork
Tilia x europaea | **Common Lime**

Avenue Length:	300m
Access:	Public

Dublin may have Chesterfield Avenue and Belfast its lime avenue to Stormont, but the 'Real Capital' has the Marina lime avenue which surpasses them all in its shimmering beauty. It has the natural advantage of running along the River Lee with beautiful Victorian mansions rising up like doll's houses on the wooded slopes of the opposite bank. Of course, this confluence of landscape beauty did not happen by accident.

In the 18th century, the growing city of Cork burst out of the confining walls of its medieval heart during a time of increased trade and prosperity to reclaim the slob lands that lay beyond. In 1760 Cork Corporation began the construction of the Navigation Wall east of the city to stop the river channel silting up with mud. Dredging of the river to give larger ships access to the city quays continued into the 19th century and the dredged-up material was deposited behind the Navigation Wall, creating reclaimed land. By 1870 the Cork Harbour Commissioners completed the project with a promenade on top of this accumulation and planted an avenue of common lime trees. In 1872 Cork Corporation formally named it 'The Marina' and it has been a favourite walk for its citizens ever since.

Beside the Marina, the reclaimed swamps now serve as the home of Cork's Gaelic games in the form of Páirc Uí Chaoimh stadium. Beyond it lies the wildfowl sanctuary, appropriately named the Atlantic Pond. The trees have done well on their diet of rich alluvial soil and while most are still intact, some trees from the original planting have been removed due to poor health or because of their roots interfering with the Navigation Wall. Go there in autumn and kick up the golden leaves while ships float by and, if you believe as I do that heaven is in the here and now, then this must be Cork's own roadway to heaven.

Cork city's lime avenue at Marina

The yew walk at Clonfert

Rag Tree at
Clonfert

Clonfert Yew Walk

Clonfert Cathedral, Clonfert, County Galway
Taxus baccata | **Yew**

HEIGHT:	15m
GIRTH:	1.5m
ACCESS:	Public

Clonfert was a monastic site founded by St Brendan the Navigator in AD 563, a couple of miles west of the River Shannon in east County Galway. This was the same St Brendan who went on a seven-year voyage across the Atlantic, and it is here that he was interred. Clonfert became a great seat of learning and sent many missions to Europe during the Dark Ages. It rivalled Clonmacnoise in importance and had up to 3,000 monks in residence. It was sacked by the Vikings several times, and the monastery was finally dissolved in the 16th century. The only remaining evidence now is the small Church of Ireland cathedral with a beautiful Hiberno-Romanesque doorway, which dates from the 12th century. The Cathedral was restored in 1664 after the sack of 1541, and it has been continually operating as a church ever since.

Beyond the cathedral lie the remains of the Bishop's Palace which was extended in 1664, and eventually sold in 1947 to Sir Oswald Mosley who was leader of the British fascists during the 1930s. He lived there until an accidental fire destroyed the palace in 1954. Before he left he donated the land that lay between the palace and cathedral to the Church of Ireland, so that the yew walk would be preserved.

The yew avenue is one of the finest and loftiest in Ireland, and the arching branches mirror the vaulting of the cathedral's roof. Reputed to be very ancient, one may visualise monks meditating and praying as they walked under its boughs. But their size and appearance suggests they are only 300 years old, at the most. The main avenue is called the 'Nuns' Walk' and is intersected midway by another incomplete avenue in a T-junction. It used to be darker and more sombre, but recent tree surgery has allowed light in and let trunks sprout new growth.

Close to the road in the woodland is a horse chestnut which in recent times has been adopted as a rag tree with numerous religious and secular objects attached to its trunk. Trees in the 21st century still have a role in people's devotional and spiritual lives.

Dean Swift's Yew Avenue

The Agri Food and Biosciences Institute, (AFBI), Loughgall, County Armagh
Taxus baccata | **Yew**

HEIGHT: 14m

GIRTH: 2.2m

ACCESS: Public during advertised opening hours : 9 a.m. – 5 p.m. (winter); 9 a.m. – 9 p.m. summer.

The great yew avenue at Loughgall Manor is still going strong 300 years after Dean Jonathan Swift used to take his daily exercise under its leaning boughs. A hawthorn at nearby Gosford was another matter though, as he ordered its removal and celebrated it with these words:

> This aged, sickly, sapless Thorn
> Which must alas no longer stand,
> Behold! the cruel Dean in Scorn
> Cuts down with sacrilegious Hand.

Swift was a friend of the Copes who bought the lands around Lough Gall in 1611 shortly after the Plantation of Ulster, and created an estate of 1,215 hectares with a manor and bawn. In 1643 it was sacked and burned during the Irish rebellion and it was not until some ten years after Cromwell had defeated the native Irish in 1651 that the English and Scottish settlements were restored. It is thought that the yew avenue dates from around 1680, when the manor was rebuilt, and forty years later Swift became familiar with it on his visits. The estate was bought in 1947 by the Department of Agriculture, and is now used as a horticultural research centre with some of the apple orchards and farmland open to the public as a country park. A visit here when the apple trees are in blossom is one of the glories of the Irish spring.

The yew avenue has several rows, creating a cathedral effect with beams of sunlight finding gaps to illuminate the columnar stems as they arch over the central path. Yews on the edge grow low and spread out creating walls of foliage so that the grove looks like a single organism when viewed from a distance.

Swift spent more time at Gosford, which is now a forest park with one of the finest arboretums in Northern Ireland, just off the main Armagh-to-Newry road. You can visit the site of what is called Dean Swift's Chair, where he used to compose verse under a yew clipped into a bower to protect him from the rain. Another yew tree at the private Glebe House next to the church in Newcastle, County Dublin, is named the 'Dean's Tree' where he used to sit while visiting, and may be the oldest tree in County Dublin at an estimated 400–500 years old. Jonathan Swift in old age greatly feared becoming mentally incapacitated, and once said, 'I shall be like that tree, I will die at the top.'

Dean Jonathan Swift (1667–1745) is said to have walked
beneath this yew avenue at Loughall Manor

Bunclody Main Street Limes

Main Street, Bunclody, County Wexford
Tilia x *europaea* | **Common Lime**

HEIGHT: 8m
GIRTH: 2.2m
ACCESS: Public

On the Carlow/Wexford boundary, where the Blackstairs Mountains slope down to the River Slaney, sits the picturesque town of Bunclody. It is named after the small River Clody, which joins the Slaney here. The town is surrounded by wooded slopes and rich farmland. For centuries it was called Newtownbarry after the large estate owned by the Barrys and on which the town grew as a source of service and labour. In the 19th century water was diverted from the millrace, which in turn was diverted from the Clody River and a little canal was built down the middle of Main Street, which became known as The Mall. The canal is lined by granite with shallow cascades and little stone bridges, while about 20 lime trees of various ages are planted alongside. It must be one of the most charming street vistas in the country: one could be transported to a French village in the blink of an eye.

The trees are not big, although some could be a considerable age. Their size is kept in check by regular pruning and pollarding. In winter they have the appearance of upturned paintbrushes and in summer they have an air of youthful exuberance. In July the scented flowers attract bees and insects in their droves, with drunken casualties littering the ground. (Honeybees and bumblebees are literally drunk from the nectar as they cannot process the high sugar levels, especially during dry or hot years.) Lime trees nourish more aphids than most, and the honeydew drips down to stain parked cars.

The Bunclody area is a hotspot for champion trees, especially on some of the old demesnes. It has a favourable microclimate in the lee of the mountains. There are a couple of woodland walks accessible to the public, and this is one of the few spots where you can find mistletoe. A good time to visit is during the festival in July, when plastic ducks race down the Mall under the lime trees. Apparently it rivals the running of the bulls in Pamplona for lunacy.

Pollarded lime trees along
Bunclody's main street

Monkey Puzzle Avenue at Woodstock

Woodstock Gardens, Inistioge, County Kilkenny
Araucaria araucana | **Monkey Puzzle**

HEIGHT: 25m
GIRTH: 4.08m
ACCESS: Public during advertised opening hours. For more information visit website: www.woodstock.ie

Monkey puzzle trees are native to the volcanic slopes of the high Andes in southern Chile. They are sometimes known as living fossils as they were one of the dominant species during the Jurassic period nearly 200 million years ago. Their spiky foliage may have been an evolutionary defence against grazing dinosaurs. Related trees found in Australia and the South Pacific demonstrate continental drift, and how those lands, along with India and Africa, once formed a supercontinent called Gondwana.

Monkey puzzles were first introduced to these islands by Archibald Menzies, a plant collector, when he pocketed five strange nuts from a dinner hosted by the Spanish Viceroy in Valparaiso in 1792. Two of them grew, but it was not until the 1840s that the tree became widely available when seed was sent back by William Lobb. The tree got its popular name when a wit declared that it would puzzle a monkey to climb it.

Monkey puzzle trees are such an alien-looking tree in our landscape that it is difficult to know where to plant them. Well, one answer is to plant them in an avenue surrounded by other trees. The finest avenue in these islands is found at the now restored gardens at Woodstock, County Kilkenny. It was planted in 1861, and consists of a quarter mile of uniformly straight trunks supporting giant umbrellas of foliage. It is as impressive an arboreal sight as you will find in Ireland, rivalled, perhaps, by the noble fir avenue 100 metres away.

Kilkenny County Council must be commended for their foresight in making Woodstock a wonderful attraction for tourists and locals alike. Now all that is needed to complete the picture are a few dinosaurs!

One of the longest and most majestic monkey puzzle avenues in Europe at Woodstock gardens

Dedicated to the memory of John Fitzgerald Kennedy, President of the United States from 1960 to 1963, the John F. Kennedy Arboretum near New Ross is a tree collection of international standing

Facing page: Eucalyptus at
John F. Kennedy Arboretum

John F. Kennedy Arboretum

New Ross, County Wexford

Access: Public during advertised opening hours

For anyone who loves trees, this is the place to visit. Established in 1968 on the slopes of Slieve Coillte, overlooking the ancestral home of John F. Kennedy, it is a fitting memorial to an inspirational figure. South Wexford is blessed by the warming influence of the Gulf Stream, with moderate rainfall and more hours of sunshine than anywhere else in Ireland. The phenological garden, which records the first leaf and flower of a variety of native shrubs and trees, shows that spring arrives in Wexford, and then moves north-west at three miles an hour before reaching Malin Head three days later. You can keep up with spring on foot if you get the timing right.

The arboretum of 250 hectares was designed and laid out by the late Tony Hanon, a forestry inspector with the then Forestry Division of the Department of Lands, and showcases over 4,000 species of trees and shrubs. Planted in groups of three, this is a living open-air encyclopaedia of all the temperate trees that can survive in Ireland. The trees are well labelled and planted together according to families. This could be regimented and dull, but it has been skilfully interwoven to create vistas, woods and parkland. Boundary shelterbelts give protection, while internal belts are removed as the arboretum matures. Forest plots are extensive and are used in research for the suitability of exotic species in Irish conditions. I particularly enjoy the eucalyptus collection, as the trees exude their oils, and you half-expect wallabies to appear. There are plenty of red squirrels about, and I heard my first Irish woodpecker here. Woodpeckers had been extinct in Ireland since medieval times due to forest clearance but recently reappeared firstly in Wicklow, having migrated across from Wales.

After over 40 years the arboretum is maturing nicely, and there are more than 100 champion trees. It has become one of the largest and best tree collections in Europe and should be enjoyed as a national treasure.

Avenue of Cedars at Tollymore

Tollymore Forest Park, Newcastle, County Down
Cedrus deodara | **Deodar Cedar**

HEIGHT:	20m
GIRTH:	4m
ACCESS:	The tree is located on private property but may be accessed during advertised opening hours. For more information visit website: www.dardni.gov.uk/forestry.

Drive through the Barbican Gate, the main entrance to Tollymore Forest Park, and you are immediately greeted by one of the most romantic avenues in Ireland. Two graceful rows of Himalayan or Deodar cedars sweep over the lawns each side of the drive, and must now be close to the visual perfection envisaged by the person who planted them, Robert Jocelyn, third Earl of Roden, Clanbrassil.

Of the four true cedar species, the Himalayan is an instant success in that it starts out as a very attractive, pendulous tree, features that are lost in its middle-aged anonymity, before it regains the dignity that comes with age and size. The Cedar of Lebanon and Blue Atlas cedar start out as shapeless bushes, before they become regal in appearance; these are the cedars you should consider if planting for yourself or your children. The Tollymore cedars were planted over 150 years ago, not long after their introduction in 1831, and it was not known how they would shape up. They come from the middle slopes of the world's highest mountains, where heavy monsoons and cool summers prepared them for life in Ireland. Typically they have a single trunk into the crown, with a nodding lead shoot that allows it to push through other species and become the dominant tree in the forest. It shares this ability with the western hemlock and Lawson cypress.

The Forest Service Northern Ireland established its first forest park here in the foothills of the Mourne mountains in 1955, and it remains the most popular in Northern Ireland, with camping, trails, forest plots and an arboretum among its attractions. There are a number of follies and bridges scattered throughout what was once the landscape park below the mansion built for the Earl of Clanbrassil. The house itself is gone, having been demolished in 1952. Its site is now a car park, and it was here that visitors got a huge shock in 1988, when a bolt of lightning struck a tall sequoia tree and shattered it to a stump, with the debris flung around the car park. That 6m-high stump remains to remind us of nature's power. The cedars have wisely kept their heads down from such potential hazards, as they usually grow tall in their native forests, which are among the most striking in the world. Their botanical name, *Cedrus deodara,* comes from the Sanskrit meaning 'Tree of the Gods' which is very appropriate.

Avenue of cedars at Tollymore Forest Park

Probably the most photographed trees in Northern Ireland, an avenue of beech trees known as the 'Dark Hedges' near Gracehill Golf Club in North Antrim

The Dark Hedges

Gracehill, Moss-Side, County Antrim
Fagus sylvatica | **Beech**

HEIGHT:	18m
GIRTH:	3.7m
ACCESS:	These trees are located along the Bregagh Road leading to Gracehill Golf Club, off local road B147.

If the oak is the king of trees then surely the beech is the queen, often called 'the lady of the woods', and the 'Dark Hedges' in North Antrim is the royal avenue of unsurpassed beauty and grace. The royal connection continues, as this avenue of beech trees used to lead to Gracehill House which was built by a James Stuart in 1775, and named after his wife.

The Stuarts were granted the lands in the early 1600s by their cousin James I who had succeeded Elizabeth I to the throne of England. The trees were planted about 200 years ago as a landscape feature on a straight avenue of half a mile which dips and rises like rolling ocean waves. It is now a public road, having become detached from the big house which now forms part of a golf club.

The original planters surely could not have imagined how the trees would stretch up and over to intertwine their smooth grey limbs and create a tunnel of shadow, light and dreamlike vision. It is not surprising that as more and more people discover them, they have become the most photographed trees in Northern Ireland, and a destination in their own right to rival Bushmills and the Giant's Causeway. Finding them may be a problem, or perhaps it just adds to the joy of discovery when you eventually come upon them in the maze of roads near Moss-side and Armoy. Get directions for Gracehill Golf Club, and you cannot be too far away.

Down the years the 'Dark Hedges' have been a favourite haunt of courting couples, but be aware that a supernatural being in the form of the 'Grey Lady' has been observed gliding along the road and disappearing after passing the last tree. Some think that she is the ghost of a maid from the big house who died mysteriously, while others think she is a tormented spirit from a nearby abandoned graveyard. Avoid visiting at Halloween as she is joined in her walk by all the other lost souls in the graveyard. Most likely it is a myth maintained by anxious fathers to prevent their daughters getting into mischief.

Broad Walk of Crimson Petals

Kilmacurragh, Kilbride, County Wicklow
Rhododendron arboretum 'Altaclarensis' | **Rhododendron**

ACCESS: Public during advertised opening hours.

Kilmacurragh could have become a byword for another fine Irish garden falling into neglect and desolation, stripped of its botanical treasures with shrugs of indifference. Scores of great gardens have come and gone, the result of one person's vision disappearing by circumstance, or the green-fingered gene skipping the next generation. But Kilmacurragh has been saved for the nation by the Office of Public Works, and new life is being breathed into its old bones: it has become an offshoot of the Botanic Gardens, Glasnevin. The house and the 2,000-hectare estate were established by the Acton family in the early 1700s. The laying-out of the grounds in the formal Dutch style of canals, avenues and wide vistas, elements of which can still be seen today, was completed in 1715 along with the completion of the Queen Anne-style house.

Successive generations of Actons planted trees in their thousands, and by the 1820s rare and exotic trees were being supplied by the famous Hodgins nursery. Thomas Acton took over the estate in 1854, and expanded the gardens into an arboretum of international renown. He formed an alliance with David Moore, curator of the National Botanic Gardens, who passed on advice and newly discovered tender trees, which were struggling in the alkaline soils of Glasnevin. Acton specialised in southern hemisphere conifers and rhododendrons from the Himalaya, amassing the most complete collection in Ireland.

The broad walk through the heart of the garden was laid out at this time, with tree rhododendrons interspersed with Irish yew. The only rhododendrons known were shrubby, until *R. arboreum* was introduced in 1820 from the Himalaya, and while it was multi-stemmed, with a height of up to 25m you could hardly deny it tree status. It was tender, but it soon hybridised with its hardier and dowdier cousins to add the glorious blood-red colour to the palette. It is one of those hybrids, called *R. arboreum* 'Altaclarensis', which today creates the magical vision in April of crimson petals raining down and carpeting the broad walk.

Thomas Acton died in 1908 and the estate passed to a nephew who died in action in the Great War, to be followed by his only brother a few months later. All the garden staff went to the bloody battlefields of France, but none came back and the estate had to be sold to pay death duties. The gardens went into steady decline until their recent rescue from the brink of extinction so that today the crimson carpet is as symbolic as the poppies of Flanders in remembering the fallen dead who worked in this great garden.

The 'Broad Walk' of rhododendrons at Kilmacurragh Gardens

The unique, mile-long avenue of giant sequoias at Emo Court

Avenue of Sequoias at Emo Court

Emo Court, Emo, County Laois
Sequoiadendron giganteum | **Wellingtonia, Giant Sequoia, Californian Redwood**

HEIGHT: 25m
GIRTH: 4.62m
ACCESS: Public during advertised opening hours.

Of the many names used for this tree – such as the Californian redwood, Wellingtonia or Mammoth tree – Giant sequoia, the name used by American foresters, is probably best in that it separates it from the other Californian redwood species, and does not offend their patriotic sensitivities. Sequoia comes from a Cherokee Indian called Sequoyah who was revered by the Native American people for creating a system of writing the Cherokee language. In the spring of 1852, a few years after his death, a hunter by the name of Augustus T. Dowd (he must have been an Irishman), made the first documented discovery of Giant Sequoias in the Sierra Nevada. Of course, it had been known as the Wawona tree by Native Americans for thousands of years, but its 'discovery' became a sensation. Seed was sent back to Ireland in 1853, and very soon every estate on these islands had one, or, in the case of Emo Court, a mile-long avenue of them, the longest in Ireland. They must have been planted by 1860, for Elwes and Henry's *Trees of Great Britain and Ireland* states in 1906 that, 'At Emo Park, in Queen's County, there is a fine avenue, though the trees are growing on poor shallow limestone soil. They are planted about 35 yards apart, and average 70 feet high by 10 feet in girth.' Most of them are still there, even though they look a bit ragged the further they are from the house, as they march across the landscape, feeling exposed without the shelter to which their ancestors were accustomed. The sequoia has proved to be tough, with the occasional loss to lightning strike and honey fungus. A big feature is the thickness of their soft bark, which helps protect them from forest fires. The heat from the fires opens the cones, which drop their seeds onto a clear seed bed of ash, making it a fire-climax tree.

Emo Court was home to the Earls of Portarlington until after the First World War, when the land was redistributed by the Land Commission, and the mansion became a centre for the Jesuit Order. One of the Jesuits, the renowned photographer Father Browne, recorded the activities on the estate during the 1930s and 1940s. The Society of Irish Foresters published a selection of the images in 1992 in *Forest Images*. The estate then came into the possession of Major Cholmeley-Harrison who presented it to the nation in 1994 after decades of restoration. Now under management of the Office of Public Works the magnificent gardens and arboretum can be enjoyed freely by the public, and the house visited for a small fee. Finally, in remembering Sequoyah it seems appropriate to recall that when the Cherokee first witnessed Europeans exchanging letters they called them 'talking leaves'.

EXOTICS

The trees (a very loose interpretation of the term, as you
will see) which feature in the following pages come with a whiff
of the desert, outback or jungle and many have the look of improbable visitors to our shores. Newly discovered lands at the ends
of the world introduced strange trees with new designs, and were
thought to be too tender to grow outdoors here. But they proved hardy
enough in our mild climate, helped by that wonderful storage heater
called the Gulf Stream washing our shores. Eucalyptus from Australia
have become huge and commonplace, while the palm-like cordyline
are ubiquitous in urban gardens. Genuine date palms from the Canary
Islands survive in Cork, while tree ferns from Australia and New
Zealand are naturalising and creating unique woodlands. I know
they are not strictly trees but some are over 6m high and cannot be
dismissed as mere plants. Other trees such as the Indian bean tree
are perfectly hardy, and with their large leaves look as if they
have strayed in from the jungle.

Canary Date Palm at Belgrove

Belgrove, Great Island, Cobh, County Cork
Phoenix canariensis | **Canary Palm**

Height: 10m
Girth: 1.91m
Access: The tree is located on private property and is not open for public access.

The date palm is the very symbol of the tropics, or an oasis in the Sahara. They are monocotyledons or a class of plants with one seed leaf, which leads to a totally different design. They don't have any real branches or annual rings of growth, and grow taller without growing thicker. All their leaves, flowers and fruit are produced from the top of the stem. Only the Chusan palm from China is reliably hardy in temperate regions, and can be seen in profusion at Huntington Castle in Carlow and the Japanese Garden in Powerscourt. But date palms growing outdoors in Ireland? Surely not! There were two at Fota near Cobh: one died at the turn of the century, while the other got killed by the big freeze in 2010. A third palm at Belgrove, a couple of miles away and, critically, a degree less frosty than Fota, has survived. There are a few in the Scilly Isles and a couple in the Channel Islands, but I am not sure if they are still alive. You will have to go a thousand miles south to see them again by the Mediterranean. The Canary Island date palm is slightly hardier than the commercial date palm of North Africa, with a magnificent broad crown and a thicker trunk. In recent years they have become popular as disposable household plants, and I was tempted to plant one out, after our run of mild winters, but along came the severe winter of 2010.

Belgrove is a private property on the east side of Great Island and was a Georgian house demolished in 1954 and replaced by a modern house. It is renowned among garden historians as the home of William Gumbleton and his garden at the close of the 19th century. Gumbleton was a rich bachelor who loved flowers and music, and was described as a small, partly bald and very pompous individual. His garden contained many rare flowers, fruit and water lilies, but sadly fell into dereliction after his death in 1911. After a hundred years of neglect and grazing animals, it is a miracle that anything survives from his planting. But among the nettles and brambles are champion walnuts, maples and Chinese cork trees. There are strange hollies waiting to be identified, and the largest Campbell's magnolia in Europe. Gumbleton was generous in distributing plants from his garden, and he donated his botanical library to the National Botanic Gardens in Glasnevin. So a solitary 10m-high spiky palm is an appropriate memorial to the remarkable man who planted it.

This 10m-high Canary date palm adds a tropical touch at Belgrove

The largest European woodland of exotic tree ferns from Tasmania at Kells Bay Gardens

Kells Bay Tree Ferns

Kells Bay Gardens, Kells, County Kerry
Dicksonia antarctica | **Tasmanian Tree Fern**

HEIGHT: 3m
GIRTH: 1.2m
ACCESS: The tree is located on private property but is open for public access during
advertised opening hours. For more information visit website: www.kellsgardens.ie.

You may wonder what business ferns have in a book about trees. *Dicksonia antarctica,* or soft tree ferns, have been a quintessential feature of Cork and Kerry gardens for over a hundred years. They are native to Tasmania, Victoria and New South Wales, and were first recorded in 1786. During the 19th-century fern mania, they became pampered denizens in fern houses. They proved to be hardy enough in mild coastal gardens of Cornwall and the south-west of Ireland, and there are reports of a shipment of tree ferns used as ballast in Kenmare Bay in the 1890s. It seems likely these were destined for Rossdohan near Sneem, as that great garden had been concentrating on plants from Australia and New Zealand for many years. They were soon passed around to other gardens in the south-west, including Derreen, Garinish, Glanleam and Kells Bay.

The trunk is made of the decaying remains of earlier growth, and forms a medium through which the roots grow. They are easily cut down, and when the top portion is replanted it will form new roots. After 20 years they produce spores and regenerate in mild, shady and damp conditions, so they soon rampaged through gardens like Kells Bay, where there is now the largest woodland of tree ferns in Europe. It is an incredible dream-like experience to tread softly among woolly trunks supporting huge umbrellas of fronds as far as the eye can see. In Australia they grow to 12m under the eucalyptus, but here they range from 1.5 to 4.5m high. Kells Bay has been under new ownership since 2006, and there has been restoration and replanting of exotic plants, including a mature Chilean wine palm as a signature centrepiece. Kells Bay has become a subtropical paradise garden by the Ring of Kerry and joins the ranks of other great coastal gardens of the south west.

A Gum Tree at Garron Point

Garron Point, County Antrim
Eucalyptus globulus | **Gum Tree**

HEIGHT: 35m
GIRTH: 7.8m
ACCESS: This tree is located on private property but is visible from Shore Road.

Garron Tower was a holiday home built in 1850 for Lady Londonderry on a plateau above the windswept Antrim coast midway between Cushendall and Carnlough. It is a severe cliff-top castle with spectacular views over the Irish Sea towards Scotland, sheltered from the west by hillside and woodland. The property became a hotel in 1915, and then in 1950 it became a Catholic grammar school, St MacNissi's College. In recent times, it amalgamated with two other schools to become a co-educational school called St Killian's.

Beside the boundary wall overhanging the road is a Tasmanian blue gum or *Eucalyptus globulus* which was planted in 1857, making it the oldest known and largest blue gum on these islands. It is 35m high and over 8m in girth, which is enormous, but which pales in comparison with the largest in Tasmania at over 90m high and up to 16m in girth. Mind you, they have had up to 600 years to become the biggest broadleaf trees in the world, along with another Tasmanian species called *Eucalyptus regnans*. The blue gum is tender and restricted to our coastline from Antrim down to Wexford and west to Kerry as 8 degrees of frost will kill it, and anyone brave enough to plant it away from these areas was caught out in the big freeze of 2010. Big trees are thriving in gardens in County Down, south Dublin and County Wicklow, and yet not one tree over 25 years old is found in Britain after heavy frosts there in 1987. Our trees survive because of the warming of the destructive easterly winds as they cross the Irish Sea.

The Garron Tower tree forks from 2m, and pushes up into a massive crown with the multicoloured bark hanging off in strips. Stand under it, close your eyes and you are immediately transported to Australia, just by the fragrant smell. The hanging sickle-shaped leaves are embellished with solitary top-shaped flower buds, which burst into creamy flowers in summer, and litter the ground in autumn. The tree was threatened with removal as it was damaging the boundary wall, but it was saved by the school bursar who realised that the wall could be replaced but that this tree could not, at least not for another 150 years.

This Tasmanian blue gum tree at Garron Point in Antrim is the oldest known and largest of its kind in Britain and Ireland

Indian Beans in Fitzgerald Park

Fitzgerald Park, Mardyke, Cork, County Cork
Catalpa x erubescens | **Hybrid Catalpa**

HEIGHT: 16m
GIRTH: 3.37m
ACCESS: Public during advertised opening hours.

In 1901 the then Lord Mayor of Cork, Edward Fitzgerald, proposed that the city stage an international industrial exhibition in the following year, and land was acquired beside the River Lee between Cork cricket grounds and what is now called Thomas Davis Bridge. It was such a great success that it was repeated in 1903, with the highlight being a visit by King Edward VII and Queen Alexandra. Fitzgerald was knighted, and the grounds were donated to Cork Corporation for use as a pleasure park by its citizens, and aptly named Fitzgerald Park. Today it is a peaceful haven, a short walk from the city centre, with a museum, cafe, sculptures and pond set among flowerbeds and lots of striking trees. Some of those trees are among the largest and finest specimens of their kind found in Ireland, such as a foxglove tree, pagoda and maple trees from the Far East, *Hoheria* from New Zealand, and Norway maples from Europe. But pride of place must go to a tree beyond the museum at the start of the river walk. It can be ignored from October through to June for it is rather gaunt and shapeless; it is the last in leaf and sheds its foliage without the benefit of any decent autumn colour. Suddenly, in midsummer, this unprepossessing yokel of the tree family bursts out in tropical gaudy oversized leaves with a purple tinge turning to lime green. It has been an aristocrat all the time waiting for the other trees to look tired and worn and then, like a preening dandy, covers itself in voluptuous white flowers. The flowers develop into pencil-thin bean pods which give us its common name of Indian bean tree. It is a member of the Catalpa genus found in North America and East Asia, and this particular tree is a hybrid from parents from those two areas called *Catalpa x erubescens,* and at 3.3m girth is a champion by some distance. Catalpas are tough and hardy and usually need hot summers to achieve any great size, so the Fitzgerald Park tree must be benefiting from the city heat island effect of bricks and tarmac radiating warmth. A five-minute walk to University College Cork campus will bring you to more great trees in the form of redwoods, black walnuts and the champion Caucasian wingnut and Chinese privet tree.

The Indian Bean Tree at Fitzgerald Park in Cork city

Strange Trees Indeed at Ilnacullin

Ilnacullin, Glengarriff, County Cork
Dacrydium cupressinum | **Rimu**

HEIGHT: 16m
GIRTH: 1.23m
ACCESS: Public during advertised opening hours.

Ilnacullin, a small island of 15 hectares in the sheltered harbour of Glengarriff in Bantry Bay, is renowned in the horticultural world as a garden of exquisite subtropical trees and shrubs. It is bathed by the warming influence of the Gulf Stream and its vegetation thrives in the mild, damp climate.

Glengarriff Bay is surrounded by beautiful wooded hills dropping down to the deep blue waters, presenting a scene of unsurpassed beauty in fine weather. The bare, rocky island was bought in 1910 by Annan Bryce, a wealthy Scottish merchant, who wanted to build a house and create a garden. He employed the English architect Harold Peto, who created the magnificent formal gardens of terraces, pool, steps and an Italian temple. In 1953, Bryce bequeathed the island to the Irish people and it is now in the care of the Office of Public Works.

There are so many wondrous trees from the Far East and southern hemisphere that it is hard to choose just one. I eventually selected a New Zealand conifer, *Dacrydium cupressinum* or a Rimu in the Maori language. It is found in Happy Valley, a long grassy glade leading to the Martello tower. A member of the Podocarp family of southern hemisphere conifers, it is a very graceful tree with long pendulous branches of light-green foliage. It was planted in the 1930s, and is now 16m high, still small compared to the few old giants of 60m still standing in their native remnant forests. Most of them were logged out by the 1960s for their valuable and handsome deep-red heartwood. An even more famous conifer from New Zealand, the Kauri pine, a member of the Araucaria family, the fourth largest tree species in the world, can be seen doing well near the Martello tower. This bare rocky island has been transformed in the space of one lifetime into a Noah's Ark of trees from around the world, a perfect paradise garden.

The pendulous branches of the rare New Zealand conifer *Dacrydium cupressinum* at Ilnacullin

Ardnagashel Myrtle Grove

Ardnagashel Lodge, Ballylickey, County Cork
Luma apiculata | **Myrtle**

HEIGHT: 12m
GIRTH: 1m
ACCESS: The tree is located on private property and is not open for public access.

Ardnagashel lies by the shore of Bantry Bay halfway between Bantry and Glengarriff. The 196-hectare estate dates back to the late 18th century, and was home to Ellen Hutchins who was widely recognised as Ireland's first woman botanist. During the 19th century it became a haven for newly introduced trees and shrubs from around the world which thrived in the warming influence of the Gulf Stream. Rhododendrons from the Himalaya, *Cryptomeria* from Japan, Podocarps and Myrtles from South America, and cork oaks reach an astonishing size and many have survived to become champions.

By the 1950s the big house was gone and the estate was split among several owners, with the arboretum and site of the original house owned by 'Rent an Irish Cottage' and the myrtle grove and coastal paths still owned by the Hutchins family. The head of the family, Richard Hutchins, 'retired' back to his ancestral home in recent years to lead family, friends and volunteers in restoring the arboretum and his beloved myrtle grove. I last met him in the pouring rain, planting rhododendrons among the myrtles when he was 95. Sadly, he passed away recently, but what a legacy he left: the most amazing woodland in these islands.

The Chilean myrtle was introduced in 1844, and first planted in Ardnagashel in 1880 where it quickly went on the rampage producing self-sown seedlings. You can see its kinship to the eucalyptus, with its flaking cinnamon-coloured bark. The leaves are small, dark and evergreen while the white scented flowers emerge in late summer. In Ardnagashel there must be 13 hectares of pure myrtle forest where the trees are drawn up to 12m, with the slim orange trunks creating a magical effect in the dappled sunlight. Native ferns and Australian tree ferns add to the enchantment. The Irish champion of 2.1m in girth is beside the lane a short distance beyond the arched entrance. Chilean myrtle seems to be a Cork speciality, as other woods are found at Castlefreke and behind the Courtmacsherry Hotel, but they cannot compare with Ardnagashel.

Chilean myrtle forms a unique woodland feature at Ardnagashel Lodge, home to Ireland's first female botanist, Ellen Hutchins (1785–1815)

Mount Usher Dombey's Beech

Mount Usher Gardens, Ashford, County Wicklow
Nothofagus dombeyi | **Dombey's Southern Beech**

HEIGHT:	34m
GIRTH:	5.12m
ACCESS:	The tree is located on private property but is open for public access during advertised opening hours. Admission charge.

Mount Usher is the jewel in the crown of Irish gardens. It brings to perfection a romantic paradise of a garden that idealises the natural world. It reflects the principles of the Irishman William Robinson who transformed the Victorian taste for formal, high-maintenance gardens. Robinson wrote the *English Flower Garden* and *The Wild Garden*, which recommended that plants be planted to reflect their natural origins, and not in the formal patterns then in vogue. His influence may be seen in other Irish gardens such as Altamont in Carlow and Annes Grove in Cork.

In 1868 Edward Walpole bought Mount Usher Mill and a few acres either side of the River Vartry. Other parcels of land were later added to bring it up to the present nine hectares. His sons took over and became gardeners of renown, one of whom built the suspension bridges over the river. The garden is protected by the Wicklow Mountains on one side, while winter cold is moderated by the Irish Sea on the other. Its acidic soil and humid climate are ideal for trees from the southern hemisphere. Mount Usher has more champion trees from Australia and South America than anywhere else in Europe. To pick one outstanding tree for this book is very much a personal choice.

The largest of three Dombey's beech, in Spanish *Coigue*, can be seen rising to 34m beyond the Palm Walk among other majestic southern beeches from Chile. Planted in 1928, it is already 5.2m in girth, and now rivals the largest in its homeland. The small, toothed evergreen leaves give a dense glossy aspect to its ascending crown. The bark is dark grey and shiny, until it matures to brown ridges which strip with age, showing orange and then dark crimson beneath. The flowers are attractive with scarlet stamens. All in all, it is the choicest evergreen broadleaf that can be grown in Ireland. Mine survived 14 degrees of frost in Carlow in 2010. Its only fault is that it grows too well, and you need space to let it be seen in all its glory.

Catherine Hutchinson is dwarfed by this impressive specimen of Dombey's southern beech at Mount Usher

CURIOSITIES

Trees come in all shapes and sizes, and grow in the most improbable of places. Curiosity is in the eye of the beholder, as I assume trees are unaware of being different or odd compared to their brethren. They just get on with the business of living wherever their embryonic seed falls, be it on a stump or high on a wall or cliff face. This extraordinary capacity for life means they are able to send roots swiftly down through cracks and find sustenance, or to grow around obstacles if they cannot swallow them first. Time-lapse photography shows plants are far from inanimate, as their leaves follow the sun, while roots and tendrils twirl and grab what they can. Trees have a different concept of time from us. Of course, humans through history have moulded trees into artistic or practical shapes as desired, epitomised by the living tree-bridges in India. We do not have anything in Ireland to rival that ingenuity, but the following pages show how Irish trees have their own way of doing things, coping with all kinds of challenges.

Hungry Tree at King's Inns

King's Inns, Constitution Hill, Dublin
Platanus x *hispanica* | **London Plane**

HEIGHT: 21m
GIRTH: 3.47m
ACCESS: The tree is located on private property but is open for public access
Monday – Friday from 7.30 a.m. – 7.30 p.m.

You would expect trees to be all bark and no bite but this remarkable London plane in the grounds of King's Inns on Constitution Hill would seem to prove the opposite. I am not sure which was there first, the cast-iron bench placed there for weary legal behinds or the estimated 80-year-old tree. The subsequent contest for space between tree and bench has proved an unequal one.

We have long known the ability of tree roots to lift and push structures around, but when faced with an object lying against it, it seems to employ the different strategy of swallowing it up. Like a beer drinker's gut hanging over his belt, this tree's ever-expanding waist has poured over the back rail of the bench. Tree bark naturally callouses over wounds to seal the cut and prevent pathogens from entering the damaged tissue. The irritation caused by the bench is being efficiently dealt with by the tree, and the tree has time on its side.

The London plane tree is a hybrid of the oriental plane from south-east Europe and the Western plane from North America. The hybrid's origin is obscure but it has been around since the 17th century. It has immense vigour, and the ability to grow in poor paved-over soil, qualities which made it a favourite for the streets of London, hence its popular name. It can withstand smog and is able to self-cleanse by shedding its bark, which gives it an attractive mottled jigsaw effect. The trunk winds its way gracefully into its airy crown of large maple-like leaves. It grows best in the fertile river valleys of the south-east where it shows its preference for summer heat. The champion of 7.3m girth may be seen at the gardens of Tourin House in County Waterford. The Hungry Tree at King's Inns is 3.5m in girth and 21m high and is not a particularly beautiful specimen, but then what can you expect when it has such a mouthful to contend with?

The 'Hungry Tree' in the
grounds of King's Inns,
Constitution Hill, Dublin

Adare Beech Swallows Headstone

St Nicholas Church, Adare, County Limerick
Fagus sylvatica | **Common Beech**

HEIGHT: 25m
GIRTH: 7.22m
ACCESS: Public

The Franciscan Friary ruins are now surrounded by the Adare Golf Club but there is public access a short walk from their car park. The friary was founded in 1464 by the Earl of Kildare and suppressed in the 16th century, only for the monks to return and be expelled during the Desmond Rebellion, and it was finally abandoned in the 1630s. The friary was known as a poor monastery, as they were dependent on alms from the community. The ruins are interesting as the church, nave, tower and cloisters are well preserved. But it is the graveyard and its attendant trees that bring us here. There are some fine yews scattered within and outside the walls, and a good three-iron shot will bring you to the Desmond castle beside the River Maigue, where there are a couple of terrific yews doing their best to compete for your attention.

The magnificent beech tree dominates the graveyard with its girth of 7m and crown almost 26m high, making it one of the greatest beech trees in Ireland – or is it? I still cannot decide if it is one, two or three trees fused together. In nature, clusters of trees germinate together as in a cache of seed forgotten by a field mouse, or deliberately sown by man to create the illusion of a wide-spreading mature tree in landscape design. One story has it that a couple of stonemasons left the headstone leaning against the tree while they went to the pub to slake their thirst, and when they returned they could not remember the location of the plot it was meant to mark. We all know how easy it is to lose the plot when the worse for wear! The headstone itself is dedicated to members of the Hourican family, with deaths recorded in 1814 and 1829. There are other good examples of headstones being swallowed at St Colmcille's Church in Swords, County Dublin and the Church of Ireland graveyard in Ballyhooly in County Cork.

A headstone is consumed by a Monterey cypress at St Colmcille's Church in Swords, County Dublin

A beech tree at St Nicholas Church in Adare is slowly swallowing the headstone of the Hourican family

Turkey-Roost Tree

Dalemount, Moone, County Kildare
Larix decidua | **European Larch**

HEIGHT: 6m

GIRTH: 2.94m

ACCESS: The tree is located on private property but is visible from the adjoining public road just outside the village of Moone in the direction of Timolin.

The common larch occurs naturally in the mountain ranges of central Europe. It is one of the few conifer trees to be deciduous; in autumn it turns a lovely soft gold, and sheds its needle leaves. In spring the leaves emerge a brilliant green, which contrasts vividly when mixed with other conifers in plantations. Foresters love it for its tough, high-quality timber, while ecologists welcome its light shade, which allows a ground layer of bluebells and other herbage to develop, which is good for insects and birds. The cones resemble wooden rose flowers when they open and the scales turn back.

Larch was introduced into Britain in the 17th century, but it only became familiar in the 1730s when the Duke of Atholl planted vast forests of it in the Scottish highlands. The oldest known tree in Ireland dates from this time, and is still to be seen at Doneraile in County Cork, but in a truncated form. Our featured tree should be familiar to anyone in the south-east who travelled the old Dublin road through the village of Moone, before it was bypassed a few years ago. It stands in the front garden of a bungalow beside a bend in the road. Behind it is a lane leading to a farmyard. Its extraordinary crown is only 6m high but nearly 24m wide. The flattened crown is not typical, but does occur occasionally. In this case its shape is explained by the tree's crown being the favourite roost of dozens of turkeys from the farm below. The combined weight of the fowl defeated the tree's attempt to grow upwards, and it had nowhere to go but out. Today the Turkey-Roost Tree seems unaware that the turkeys are long gone.

The unusually flattened crown of the Turkey-Roost Tree near Moone

Packhorse-Bridge Tree, Coolaney

Coolaney Bridge, Coolaney, County Sligo
Fagus sylvatica | **Common Beech**

HEIGHT: 14m
GIRTH: 2.35m
ACCESS: This tree is located on private property and is not open for public access.

Coolaney is a pretty little village in the lee of the Ox Mountains, as they drop towards Ballysadare Bay near Sligo Town. Not to be confused with Colloney a few miles away on the N4, this village is perched beside the Owen Beg River as it plunges seawards. The remains of an old mill beside the beautiful riverside walk are part of its industrial heritage, along with the disused railway which finally closed in 1976.

A neglected feature of Coolaney's heritage is the packhorse bridge hidden away downriver in a wooded glen. Before the advent of railways, canals and the turnpike roads of the 18th and 19th centuries, Ireland had very poor communications and most travel was on foot or by packhorse. Typically packhorse bridges were designed with low parapets so as to not interfere with the horse's panniers, and triangular recesses to give refuge to pedestrians. Long-distance travel was limited and tracks and paths evolved to follow the line of least resistance as they twisted and turned to avoid poorly drained areas. The packhorse bridge in Coolaney would have been part of that network until the railway between Tuam and Sligo was completed in 1895, which left the bridge neglected and forgotten.

Access to the bridge is almost impossible and this tree, which grows on the bridge, is best seen from the riverbed during a dry spell. It is an incredible sight looking up at the beech tree over the central arch which stands 9m above the river with the tree another 12m higher again. It is an astonishing location for a tree but sadly the masonry is falling into the river as the roots undermine the bridge and action needs to be taken now or both will tumble into the abyss.

A beech tree perches
precariously on the packhorse
bridge at Coolaney

An old ash tree envelops the remains of
Lissanover Castle in County Cavan

Castle One Tree

Bawnboy, County Cavan
Fraxinus excelsior | **Ash**

HEIGHT:	17m
GIRTH:	7.29m
ACCESS:	The tree is located on private property. Viewing is by prior appointment only.

'Castle One Tree' is a recently coined name given to an incredible old ash tree which is gorging on what remains of Lissanover Castle between Bawnboy and Templeport. Lissanover translates from Irish as the 'Fort of Pride', and the story goes that one of its occupants had a priest murdered at the altar because he had started Mass without him. In medieval times the castle was a stronghold of the ruling McGovern clan, and commanded views of the Barony of Templeport from Fermanagh to the Shannon basin as it fed into Lough Allen. Another account translates Lissanover as 'Fort of Extravagance'; in this version a Baron McGovern was building the castle and had his tenants drive their cows to be milked at the castle every day, and the produce was used instead of water to make the mortar. Bullocks' blood was also used, and if anyone refused, the Baron had them hanged. The McGoverns' despotic rule did not survive the Elizabethan plantation, and the castle stone was recycled into the construction of Lissanover House in the 18th century. By the early 20th century, the mansion had suffered the same fate as the castle, and its stone was reused in the building of local farmers' homes after the estate was divided up by the Land Commission.

Permission to view the tree from Martin Donohoe on whose land the tree stands is essential, as the grazing bullocks may have an ancestral memory of what happened to their forebears. Climb the hill until it levels off, and only bumps and hollows remain of the fort, except for the stout ash on its pedestal of stone. The trunk is over 7m in girth although it is not a conventional trunk, as many roots drop down from the original height of the wall where the ash seeded itself some 300 years ago. The tree's height and spread is over 18m, and it is obviously thriving on its diet of blood and milk. It is clear why this tree was left well alone, for who knows what malevolent spirit might be released if it is interfered with? The McGoverns had the habit of imprisoning their opponents in wooden barrels with nails driven in and rolling them down the hill from this castle.

Grasping Birch of Sandyford

Burton Hall, Sandyford, Dublin
Betula pendula | **Silver Birch**

HEIGHT: 14m
GIRTH: 3.23m
ACCESS: This tree is located on private property and is not open for public access.

If the island of Ireland were evacuated and abandoned to nature, there would soon be a forest of birch and willow trees marching across the landscape. Birch are the ultimate pioneers, with their lightweight seed blowing far in the wind, or dispersed by the finches and blue tits building up reserves of fat for the winter. They colonised Ireland about 11,000 years ago and dominated the landscape for thousands of years before oak, elm and pine eventually shaded them out. Ireland has two native species, the silver birch and the downy birch, which resemble each other to such an extent that you need to be able to count their chromosomes in a lab in order to identify them reliably. In my experience I find the silver birch to have more elegant arched branches than the shapeless crown of the downy birch. Birch is renowned for its silvery white bark, which darkens in old age (which may be as little as 80 years). They live fast and die young, apart from stunted trees at higher altitudes such as those in Killarney National Park. Their feminine beauty is enhanced in autumn when their leaves turn to pure gold with only the aspen as a rival among our native trees.

Our featured tree demonstrates a birch tree's amazing opportunism in seeding itself on top of a tree stump in the garden of Burton Hall, right in the heart of Sandyford Industrial Estate. The old house dates from 1741 and is now used as a community mental health services centre called Cluain Mhuire, under the patronage of the Hospitaller Order of St John of God. The restored walled garden may be visited on Wednesday afternoons. Dublin's largest tree, a Monterey cypress with a girth of 10.6m, dominates the grounds. But it is the sight of the birch bestriding the large stump like a spider gorging on its prey which will leave one fearing that the triffids have arrived among us. Dismiss those negative thoughts with Samuel Taylor Coleridge's often quoted words from 'The Picture of the Lover's Resolution':

> And hark, the noise of a near waterfall !
> I pass forth into light – I find myself
> Beneath a weeping birch (Most beautiful
> Of forest trees, the Lady of the Woods)

A self-sown birch tree grows from a stump at Burton Hall, Sandyford

St Mary's Well, Rosserk

Rosserk Abbey, Ballina, County Mayo
Crataegus monogyna | **Hawthorn**

HEIGHT: 2m
GIRTH: 0.45m
ACCESS: This tree is located on private property which is open to public access.

A couple of kilometres north of Killala, by the mouth of the River Moy, signposts draw you to Rosserk Abbey which was founded by the Franciscans in about 1440. It is situated by the estuary, and is extolled as one of the most beautiful ruined abbeys in the country. It was created for a community of married people who were unable to be become nuns and monks but still wanted to adopt the monastic life. Just over half a kilometre before the abbey, another sign directs you to Tobermurray, or St Mary's Well, and a five-minute walk brings you to a grassy hollow with a stream dropping down to a sheltered sea inlet. That stream emerges from a spring at the bottom of a slope where an apparition of the Virgin Mary is said to have occurred in 1680. It is likely that St Mary's Well was used for Mass during the penal times of the 18th century. A tiny stone vaulted chapel with a cross over the well has an inscription in Latin which reads, 'this chapel was built in honour of the Blessed Virgin in the year of our Lord 1798 by John Lynott of Rosserk, Esq'. The well was venerated and people came to pray, seek cures and leave offerings. It was particularly noted for the cure of bad eyesight, and devotees washed their eyes and drank the water. Pattern day is on 15 August, when Mass is held.

What makes the shrine special is the presence of a small hawthorn growing out of the stone roof, with no appearance of roots, inside or out, connecting with the ground. Locals say that it first appeared about a hundred years ago, but there are no legends associated with its appearance, apart from the miracle of surviving in such an exposed and hungry place. It is 2m tall and 0.45m in girth, and had a fine crop of haws when I visited. It must be especially lovely garlanded in May blossom. There are other extraordinary trees growing in unusual places featured in this book, but this one beats them all.

A hawthorn tree grows out of a stone roof at St Mary's Well, Rosserk

Drenagh Sycamore with a Twist

Drenagh, Limavady, County Derry
Acer pseudoplatanus | **Sycamore**

HEIGHT: 26m
GIRTH: 3.93m
ACCESS: The tree is located on private property. Viewing is by prior appointment only.

Drenagh is a magnificent wooded estate near the town of Limavady between Derry and the north Antrim coast. The McCausland family have been here over 300 years and built the present mansion in 1837. The McCauslands can trace their ancestry back a thousand years to Anselan O'Cahan, who successfully used the strategy of dressing up in women's clothes to surprise and slaughter his Viking oppressors. The family's resourcefulness continues in the landscaping of the parkland with sweeping views of Binevenagh Mountain framed by mature trees beyond the lawn terraces. A working walled garden, Italian garden and moon garden along with imposing conifer specimen trees beside the river add to the beauty of the estate, and may be enjoyed by wedding guests and conference visitors.

The tree I wish to bring to your attention is a sycamore near the house of such beauty in form and proportion that it could bring a Road-to-Damascus conversion to conservationists who wish to remove this maligned species from our hedges and woodlands. The trunk leans and spirals to nearly 12m before the first branch and appears to be made of numerous columns rising from root to branch independently but bound with a sharing of the crown's load. The crown rises over 26m in perfect symmetry and balance, making me wonder if Mr McCausland, who used to be a tree surgeon, might be spending an awful lot of time pruning and preening the tree. A second large gnarly sycamore in the park is the very antithesis of the handsome spiral tree. It is over 6.4m in girth around its knobbly waist, and it soon swells into many stems with enough nooks and crannies to house a clattering of jackdaws. Talk about beauty and the beast!

Conservationists should give the sycamore some slack as it harbours vast quantities of aphids, and attracts bees to its spring nectar. It is native to the mountains of Central Europe which is a long way from any sea, and yet no native tree can rival its ability to withstand exposure and provide shelter around our coast.

The spiralling trunk of a
sycamore at Drenagh

TREES ASSOCIATED WITH A PERSON

The Americans who conserved the mighty sequoias had the right idea when they named their colossal giants after generals and presidents. No patriot in their right mind would dare harm a tree associated with such personages. Maybe we should take a leaf out of their book, and name prominent trees after our sporting and cultural heroes? As it is, one winner in Irish history had several trees named after him and the King William chestnut in Scarva still survives. Such trees tell a story of historical events, and are a living memorial to remarkable people. Some trees have recently died, the Brian Boru yew in Clontarf, for example, while others like the Walter Raleigh yews in Youghal are inaccessible to the public. Also included in this section are witness trees that have seen gruesome events in our past. If you live long enough you see the best and worst of human behaviour: just as well that trees can't talk.

Left: Lady Gregory's Autograph Tree, a copper beech in the walled garden at Coole Park
Top right: The trunk is enclosed by a metal fence to prevent damage
Bottom right: Some of the famous initials carved into Coole Park's Autograph Tree. (1. Sculptor and medallion portrait artist Theodore Spicer-Simson; 2. Playwright George Bernard Shaw; 3. Poet John Masefield; 4. Countess of Cromartie; 7. Celtic scholar, poet and president of Ireland, An Craoibhín Aoibhinn (Douglas Hyde); 9. William Robert Gregory, son of Lady Augusta Gregory.)

The Autograph Tree

Coole Park, Gort, County Galway
Fagus sylvatica Atropurpurea Group | **Copper Beech**

HEIGHT: 21m
GIRTH: 3.5m
ACCESS: Public

During the early 20th century Coole Park was the home of Lady Gregory, the dramatist and co-founder of the Abbey Theatre, and there she entertained many people associated with the Irish Literary Revival.

W. B. Yeats in 'Coole Park 1929' wrote:

> Here traveller, scholar, poet, take your stand,
> When all these rooms and passages are gone,
> When nettles wave upon this shapeless mound,
> And saplings root among the broken stone.'

Unfortunately these words foretold the demise of the house at Coole Park, as it was allowed to fall into a state of neglect after Coole was sold to the state before Lady Gregory died. Thankfully, her beloved woods and walled garden where she loved to sit under her favourite Catalpa tree are well looked after nowadays and enjoyed by the public.

She wrote, 'I have gone far out in this world, east and west in my time, and so the peace within these enclosing walls is fitting for the evening of my days.' The walled garden is also home to the 'Autograph Tree', which playwright Sean O'Casey described: 'Away in a sacred spot of the garden, a magnificent copper beech swept the ground with its ruddy branches, forming within them a tiny dingle of its own. This was the sacred tree of Coole. On its trunk were carved the initials of famous men so that they may be remembered for-ever. The initials of Augustus John were there, and those of Bernard Shaw and Yeats were cut deep into the bark that looked like hardened dark-red velvet'.

In 1898, Lady Gregory invited W. B. Yeats to initial the smooth stem. Other famous people who also carved their initials on the tree include Yeats' brother Jack, George Bernard Shaw, John Masefield and Sean O'Casey. While years of growth have altered some carvings, most are still legible today. The trunk is now enclosed by a metal fence to prevent any damage to this special tree. There are many other wonderful trees in the park, with the main avenue of holm oaks and the largest oriental plane in Ireland close to the site of the demolished house. Sean O'Casey in his memoir wrote, 'Books and trees were Lady Gregory's chief charmers, the one nearest her mind, the other nearest her heart. She laboured long and lovingly in the woods of Coole.'

Bishop Bedell's Sycamore

Kilmore Cathedral, Kilmore, County Cavan
Acer pseudoplatanus | **Sycamore**

HEIGHT: 17m
GIRTH: 7.42m
ACCESS: Public

Back in 1833 James Rennie wrote in *The Field Naturalist*: 'There is in this neighbourhood a noble tree, memorable as well on its own account, being an uncommon specimen of its kind, as from local circumstances, which are likely to make it equally an object of interest to many of your readers. I allude to a sycamore, in the garden of the Bishop's residence at Kilmore, about three miles from Cavan.' The tree is known as Bishop Bedell's sycamore, and tradition tells us that it was the first planted in Ireland in 1632. It stands close to the bishop's tomb behind the graveyard walls of Kilmore Cathedral. Bedell was born in Essex and came to Ireland in 1627, when he became provost of Trinity College Dublin. He was then consecrated Church of Ireland Bishop of Kilmore and Ardagh, and, although full of Reformation zeal, he was supportive of the local population as hostilities intensified against England and its policies. War broke out in 1641, and Bedell gave sanctuary to all persuasions at Kilmore, but was eventually captured and held prisoner by local warlords. He died from typhus soon after release in 1642, and is best remembered for initiating the first translation of the Bible into Irish.

In 1833, James Rennie measured the tree to be 14ft 6ins (4.4m) in girth at its waist three feet above the ground. A hundred years later it measured 21ft (6.4m) and now is 24ft (7.31m) girth. Rennie also describes a massive branch of 11ft (3.35m) girth which 'passes off laterally in an angle, and, overhanging the adjoining church-yard, forms a canopy for Bedell's tomb'. Unfortunately, that limb split and came tumbling down about 20 years ago, leaving a large gaping hole in the trunk. Let us hope the tree continues to battle against the elements and that we can celebrate its 400th anniversary in 20 years' time. There are several even more imposing sycamores by the avenue leading up to the cathedral which will in time continue to grace this, the high altar of the sycamore in Ireland.

Bishop Bedell's sycamore at
Kilmore Cathedral

The majestic 'Brian Boru Oak' in east Clare

Brian Boru Oak

Raheen Woods, Tuamgraney, County Clare
Quercus petraea | **Sessile Oak**

HEIGHT: 25m
GIRTH: 7.96m
ACCESS: The tree is located on private property. Viewing is by prior appointment only.

The Brian Boru oak is one of the most celebrated and best-known trees in Ireland and postcards have been sold with its image. No other tree has been honoured in this way. It is associated with Brian Boru who was born nearby and who became High King of Ireland a thousand years ago. He defeated the Dublin Norse and the Uí Neills of Ulster at the Battle of Clontarf in 1014, but died in battle as he ended the Uí Neills' domination of the High Kingship of Ireland.

Some claim that the tree itself is a thousand years old and might have been planted by Brian Boru. Unfortunately, this fanciful notion gets repeated by the media and tourist brochures and is accepted as fact without any hard evidence. Assumption is the mother of invention, and I have been guilty of it with this tree. I first paid respects to this aristocrat one winter, and mistakenly identified it as a common oak. Common oaks have basal leaf lobes on a short stalk, with a long stalk for its acorns, while sessile oaks have wedge-shaped leaves on a long stalk, and no stalk for its acorns. The Brian Boru is known to be a sessile oak, as are most of the oaks in Raheen Woods nearby. A combination of genetic and pollen studies have shown that our native oaks migrated from their refuge in the Iberian Peninsula after the ice retreated. This area of Clare was renowned in medieval times for the wild woods of Suidain which stretched from the Slieve Aughty mountains down to Lough Derg. They were eventually laid waste for charcoal production, and Raheen Woods and its largest tree are a surviving remnant.

To visit the oak please get permission from its owner, William McLysaght, who runs a nursery at the entrance to the old Raheen Manor estate. Follow a muddy lane at the back of Raheen Community Hospital grounds through woodland until you reach a field on the right. There the tree stands in all its magnificence. It has an immense fluted and ridged trunk almost 8m in girth which forks 2m above ground into a massive wide crown over 25m high. It certainly looks ancient, and is a much more impressive and photogenic tree than its rival up the road in Mountshannon. It could be anywhere between 300 to 500 years old, and let us hope it eventually reaches 1,000 years.

The Ilchester Oak

Glenstal Abbey, Murroe, County Limerick
Quercus petraea | **Sessile Oak**

HEIGHT: 19m
GIRTH: 5.88m
ACCESS: The tree is located on private property. Viewing is by prior appointment only.

In the grounds of Glenstal Castle once stood Cappercullen House, the home of the O'Gradys, an old and honoured family in the 18th century. The only child, a daughter called Mary, was one of the brightest and most beautiful women in the country. It was at a ball in Limerick when she was 17 that she first met Lord Stavordale, the oldest son and heir of Lord Ilchester, one of the richest men in England. He was stationed in Limerick with his regiment, and fell in love at first sight with Mary. He took every opportunity to visit, and to court her beneath the tree she swung from as a child.

Mary's father, seeing how the romance was blossoming and concerned that her affection would be misplaced as surely Lord Ilchester would object to his son marrying the daughter of a poor Irishman, wrote to Lord Ilchester warning him of the situation, and pleading with him to remove his son for everyone's good. Lord Ilchester replied, thanking him, and said that his agent would call to thank him in person. Months later the agent arrived, and was invited to stay the week. He was charmed by Mary's beauty and good manners, but was concerned about her health and depression. Mr O'Grady told him that it was because she had had no contact with her beau, but that she would get over it, and not to tell Lord Ilchester about any of this. The agent replied that he was Lord Ilchester, and had come in disguise, and would be delighted for his son to take Mary as his wife. And so they were wed and spent many happy years together.

Cappercullen House was replaced by Glenstal Castle in the mid-19th century, and in 1928 it became a boarding school and Benedictine Abbey. The old trysting oak can be seen by the drive opposite the first lake. It looks every inch its 300-odd years. It is 5.8m in girth, but lost a large trunk from the base, leaving a substantial cave in which to shelter from the elements. Nearby there are many other elderly sessile oaks, thought to be remnants of an ancient forest. There is a magnificent glen for walking and contemplation, and superb exotic trees and rhododendrons scattered through the grounds. The monks take great care of the gardens and are very welcoming and knowledgeable.

The Ilchester oak at Glenstal Abbey tells a romantic tale

The Silken Thomas Yew at St Patrick's College, Maynooth

Silken Thomas Yew

St Patrick's College, Maynooth, County Kildare
Taxus baccata | **Yew**

HEIGHT:	14m
GIRTH:	6.2m
ACCESS:	The tree is located on private property but is open for public access. It can be viewed just inside the entrance to St Patrick's College on the left-hand side.

If pushed to the pin of my collar, I would have to say that this tree has more reasons than most to claim the title of Ireland's oldest tree. There have been repeated claims down the centuries that it was planted at the same time that Maurice FitzGerald built his castle in 1176. The Earls of Kildare became the most powerful Anglo-Norman family in medieval times. Between 1487 and 1513, the eighth Earl governed Ireland on behalf of the English Crown. His son Gerald, the ninth Earl, was summoned to London in 1534 to answer charges of treason. Enemies of the FitzGeralds spread false rumours that he had been executed, which prompted his son Thomas to revolt, and he and his horsemen rode into Dublin with silken ribbons on their helmets, hence his name. They were repulsed in their attack on Dublin Castle, and they withdrew to his castle in Maynooth. Later this castle was besieged by English forces, using artillery for the first time in Ireland. Thomas negotiated his safety, and on the night before his surrender he played his harp under the spreading branches of the old yew, which had sheltered generations of his forefathers, for the last time. That does seem unlikely considering his plight. Thomas and five of his uncles were sent to the Tower of London and executed at Tyburn.

In 1795, following the abolition of the Penal Laws, the Maynooth castle was offered to the Catholic Church as the location of the first seminary to be founded in Ireland. This was not entirely altruistic, as it was feared that priests trained in France could bring back revolutionary ideas. In 1884 it was reported that ghosts had been observed dancing between the two large yew trees. In 1897 John Lowe, author of *Yew Trees of Britain and Ireland* measured the yew at 20ft/6m in girth, the largest then in Ireland. By 1945 the spreading low branches were considered a nuisance and removed, which is a great shame as they were essential to the tree's ability to stand up to storms. Ancient trees which have had too much care lose their gnarly character and presence. It is impossible to verify its age by carbon dating or taking core samples, as it has been hollow for a long time. Yew trees of comparable size and appearance in Britain with proven historical data would suggest that the Silken Thomas yew could be between 700 and 1,200 years old. The matching yew on the other side of the central path is a fine tree in its own right, with a girth of 4.9m. Nearby is one of the largest specimens of a Tree of Heaven, *Ailanthus altissima*, in Ireland, with its compound leaves – a rather apt tree for a seminary.

Lord Rossmore's Tree

Rossmore Forest Park, Monaghan, County Monaghan
Sequoiadendron giganteum | **Giant Redwood**

HEIGHT: 44m
GIRTH: 6.54m
ACCESS: The tree is located on property owned by Coillte and is open for public access in accordance with the company's open-forest policy.

Rossmore Forest Park is situated a couple of miles outside Monaghan on the Newbliss Road. The 524 hectares lie in the heart of drumlin country, which defines the 'basket of eggs' topography of south Ulster. The forest park was created on the old estate of Rossmore Castle after it was sold in 1950 to the state. The huge late-Georgian mansion became uninhabitable after the Second World War due to dry rot, and was eventually demolished in 1974. You can admire the same views that former Lords Rossmore enjoyed, the rolling countryside of lake and hills, from the embankments of the hilltop house site in the middle of the park. The then Forest and Wildlife Service conserved the remaining trees, and reforested open parkland to turn it into a popular amenity for walkers. The park is now managed by Coillte and there is also coarse fishing in its lakes. Many of the old landscape features remain, including the walled garden, yew avenue and exotic trees.

A modest obelisk records the planting of the tree by Henry Cairnes Westenra, fourth Lord Rossmore, on his 11th birthday in 1862.

Sequoias and other huge old conifers line the entrance avenue with an under-storey of rhododendrons, which flower profusely in early summer. Many of these trees have their own small headstones which detail the species and planting date, and indicate the pride and importance of these newly introduced trees to major landowners in the 19th century. Like racehorses, trees became a competitive sport among neighbouring landowners – to have the first or largest of a species – and the sequoia became the most prized tree soon after its discovery in 1853. Lord Rossmore's competitive spirit is demonstrated by the fact that he had his drawing room expanded five times in a competition with Mr Shirley of Lough Fea as to who could claim the largest room in County Monaghan.

Beyond the yew avenue near Priestfield Lake, look for the towering sequoia among the younger plantations. It is known as Lord Rossmore's tree, and at 44m high is the tallest tree in Monaghan. The headstone states that it was planted in 1862, and hopefully the tree will thrive for hundreds of years to come and remain a fitting memorial to the man. But the champion sequoia, girthing 0.9m larger, is in the Shirley estate at Lough Fea. I wonder who is having the last laugh.

A giant redwood planted by Lord Rossmore in 1862 is the tallest tree in Monaghan at 44m high

The Birdy Tree

Shercock Road, Carrickmacross, County Monaghan
Aesculus hippocastanus | **Horse Chestnut**

HEIGHT:	10m
GIRTH:	3.07m
ACCESS:	This tree is visible alongside the R178 public road.

The 'Birdy Tree' is a horse chestnut at a junction on the Shercock Road out of Carrickmacross. It was a landmark and meeting place, especially for cattle dealers and young fellows who used to dam up the nearby stream and turn it into a swimming pool. One day back in 1968 Michael Birdy came upon county council workers busy digging clay from around the base, cutting the roots and attempting to push it over with a digger. Michael stopped the digger and telephoned George Cannon who was the County Manager at the time. The digger pushed the chestnut back to the vertical and local men shovelled clay back over the roots in an attempt to save the tree. Mr Birdy jokes that they were the original eco-warriors, and that it was just something that had to be done. Another attempt was made by the council to push it over a few days later but thankfully the digger broke down. Before Mr Birdy's intervention, a photographer from the local newspaper, *Northern Standard,* took a picture of the damaged tree and the headline that week was 'This is the last of the old trees at McCarthney's Cross before they removed it'. One week later the headline ran 'The tree at McCarthney's Cross is still there'!

In the meantime the County Manager called off the workers and wrote to Mr Birdy stating that the tree had been so badly damaged, it could fall but that they would wait and see what happened. Soon afterwards the tree came back into life and the buds burst forth. The tree is still hale and hearty, and is loved and appreciated to this day. Mr Birdy and the County Manager should be congratulated for saving it. The lesson for all of us who love trees is that you can make a difference and should be vigilant for all trees that are threatened in your community.

The 'Birdy Tree' is a landmark horse chestnut tree at Carrickmacross

King William's Chestnut, Scarva

Scarva House, Scarva, County Down
Castanea sativa | **Sweet Chestnut**

HEIGHT: 13m
GIRTH: 8.52m
ACCESS: The tree is located on private property and is not open for public access.

In June 1690 King William III and an army of 30,000 men first rendezvoused and camped at Scarva before pushing on to battle against King James II's forces at the River Boyne in County Meath. Scarva House was built in 1717 on lands granted by King William to John Reilly, in recognition of services rendered to the Crown, and the period house stands today little changed, overlooking charming, rolling parkland beside the Newry Canal which divides Armagh from Down. It is now a private stud farm, but it may be visited on 13 July when with tens of thousands of visitors assemble for the annual 'Sham Fight' which re-enacts the Battle of the Boyne, and celebrates King William's stay at Scarva. It is a festive occasion, without the political overtones and religious tensions of the Twelfth, or Orangeman's Day.

At Scarva there is a living link with William of Orange in the form of a magnificent sweet chestnut on the lawn near the house. It seems that he tied his horse to various trees on his journey south to his appointment with King James's army, and all have died in the intervening centuries. There was even a 'Royal Oak' in Fermanagh, which was quite a detour!

The Scarva chestnut has the strongest link of all, and its incredible shape of many trunks erupting from a short bole is explained by the story of William's horse treading on it when tethered to the tree. Massive branches stretch out dead and debarked, exposing whorls of beautifully patterned grain. One branch is propped, while others are perfectly healthy, carrying dense foliage high into the crown. This two-sides-of-the-one-coin effect is typical of the sweet chestnut's ability to renew itself even in old age by sending up new shoots, with branches resting on the ground and putting down roots. A sweet chestnut on the slopes of Mount Etna in Sicily is reckoned to be nearly 2,000 years old and only the yew and olive tree have the potential to live that long, among European trees. Long may this tree live to see the history and symbols that divide the people of Ireland made redundant.

King William's Chestnut at Scarva House

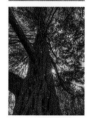

AMERICAN GIANTS

The new world initally proved to be an inconvenient barrier to the riches of the Orient but it soon provided unique riches of its own, with its gold, silver and new products such as maize, potatoes and tobacco. It was the same with trees and the introduction of North American trees reflects the westward expansion and colonisation of that great continent from the 17th to the 19th centuries. The first thing to remember is that the continent is divided by great climatic and physical barriers, including the Rocky Mountains, and hardly any one species is found across the entire continent. The north–south orientation of the mountains meant that trees could migrate south during the Ice Age, and then migrate back when the ice retreated. None of those trees was lost, so today we have a huge number of broadleaf trees in the eastern United States, and numerous conifers in the west. The earliest trees to arrive in Ireland were eastern broadleafs such as red oak, robinia, magnolias, maples and the tulip tree. Many of the eastern trees survived in Ireland, but did not thrive, as they needed hotter summers. We had to wait until the 19th century, and the introduction of the giant conifers from the temperate rainforests of the northwest for American trees to find a true 'home from home' here, as the following pages illustrate.

Tallest Tree in Ireland

Powerscourt, Enniskerry, County Wicklow
Pseudotsuga menziesii | **Douglas Fir**

HEIGHT:	61.5m
GIRTH:	5.3m
ACCESS:	This tree is located in the grounds of Powerscourt Estate which are open to the public. For more information visit website: www.powerscourt.ie

Powerscourt is the great showpiece of Irish gardens in a sublime setting in the Wicklow Hills, with superb views of the Sugarloaf Mountain. Terraced gardens on a grand scale drop down to a circular lake, with a background of mostly conifer trees and rare broadleaves enhancing the experience for tree enthusiasts. Beyond, the ground slopes down to the Dargle River which meanders through the estate, having caught its breath after its tumultuous drop over the highest waterfall in Ireland. The Dargle Valley, with its riverside walk constructed in 1871, is open to the public on an annual membership scheme, and to guests staying at the Ritz-Carlton hotel on the estate. Hotel guests certainly are very privileged, having access to glorious woodland trails, and Ireland's own 'Avenue of Giants' that rivals all other contenders in Europe.

The seventh Viscount Powerscourt went on a spree in the 1860s and 1870s, at the height of conifer mania, planting sequoia, Sitka spruce, Monterey cypress and Corsican pine that all now reach heights of 40 to 50m on the sheltered floor of the valley. The grove containing over a hundred monkey puzzle trees would be the perfect location for a Spielberg dinosaur film.

Near the end of the 3km walk approaching Weir's Lodge, the trees get even taller, as those aristocrats of the conifer family, Douglas firs, look down on their American siblings. The tallest of all at 61.5m (202ft), has been Irish champion for the last 20 years, overtaking two co-champion Sitka spruce in Shelton Abbey and Curraghmore. It has a superb slim spire, best seen from a distance on a bend before the avenue enters the final straight. Walk in to its base, and the corky cylindrical trunk just goes up and up, reaching for the clouds. But it is only a child compared to the tallest living Douglas fir in Oregon at 100m high. Only the coastal redwood in California, at 115m, is taller again, though in the past there are strong claims for felled Douglas firs reaching 120m. Most of the wild stands are gone, as it proved to be very strong timber, yielding huge quantities of straight poles. Replanted forests of Douglas fir are still the main source for the lumber industry in the western parts of North America.

The champion at Powerscourt might not retain its status for much longer, as younger Douglas fir in Avondale are catching up fast, but a re-measure in the summer of 2013 by John Dempsey of Coillte using the latest laser technology confirms that this tree is the first to surpass 60m (or 200ft) in Ireland.

The tallest tree in Ireland is a Douglas fir, at Powerscourt Estate in County Wicklow. This tree measures 61.5m in height

Curraghmore Sitka Spruce

Curraghmore, Portlaw, County Waterford
Picea sitchensis | **Sitka Spruce**

HEIGHT: 55m

GIRTH: 6.91m

ACCESS: This tree is located on private property which is open for public access during advertised opening hours. For more information visit website: www.curraghmorehouse.ie

Sitka spruce plantations have a bad reputation in Ireland. They look like giant caterpillars munching their way across our bogs and hillsides, and are dismissed as sterile blocks of ugly green aliens. This effect can be improved by mixed planting, especially of broadleaves around the edges. What cannot be denied is that Sitka outgrows and out-yields every other tree on poor, wet degraded land, and that Ireland needs forestry. Some of our threatened wildlife, such as pine martens and hen harriers, have increased in number as a consequence. Sitka spruce was introduced by David Douglas in 1832 from the Pacific Northwest coast of America. The largest spruce in the world, these 90m monsters can be found in the temperate rainforest of Vancouver Island. Only two authentic trees from this introduction are known: one in Abbeyleix, and our featured tree in one of the handsomest of Irish demesnes, Curraghmore. It was planted in 1835 high up beside St John's Bridge. By 1974 this tree, at 49m tall, along with another Sitka in Shelton Abbey, was competing to be the tallest tree in Ireland. It is now 55m but was surpassed by a Douglas fir 20 years ago in Powerscourt, which is now 61.5m.

Stand under this tree and admire the presence and vitality of its trunk, buttressed by huge surface roots. The effect of its emerging green buds against the blue-green needles in May is especially striking. A few years ago it lost all its leaves through aphid infestation, and I feared for its future. It recovered well and looks good for another two centuries or so. Nearby are found other Sitkas, redwoods and some of the finest Scots pine in the country. That Douglas fir in Powerscourt had better not get too uppity. You know what can happen to tall poppies.

This Sitka spruce at Curraghmore House and Gardens is one of only two originals remaining from David Douglas' 1830s introduction to Ireland.

Tempo Manor Champion Spruce

Tempo Manor, Tempo, County Fermanagh
Picea sitchensis | **Sitka Spruce**

HEIGHT: 52m
GIRTH: 5.52m
ACCESS: The tree is located on private property and is not open for public access.

The tallest tree in Northern Ireland at 52m now stands at Tempo Manor beside the village of Tempo, a few miles east of Enniskillen. It has only claimed the crown in the last few years, as the previous champion, also a Sitka spruce, at Caledon in County Tyrone, formerly 54.25m, has died back to 51.5m. Such is the snakes-and-ladders effect of measuring tall trees, and the risk trees take when poking their heads above everything else, and exposing themselves to the elements. A bit like us humans, where it seems height is temporary and girth permanent, at least in my personal experience.

Tempo Manor is a 200-hectare private estate which hosts weddings and corporate events. If you get an invitation, it will allow you to admire the wonderful champion spruce beside the main drive, as it weaves by the river and natural lakes. The present house was built in 1863 overlooking the splendid landscaped park, lake and woodland. It was the seat of the Maguires who as local chieftains were one of the few Gaelic families to hold on to their estates through the turbulent 17th-century wars, and were compelled to convert in order to keep their lands under the Penal Laws. In the mid-18th century, the legendary villain Hugh Maguire imprisoned his wife in the old castle when she refused to give up her jewellery and the title deeds to her English estate. No one interfered, as he was a renowned duellist. After many years she finally revealed where these were hidden, and Hugh in his rush to open her secret compartment cut himself badly and died in agony from tetanus. His wife was then released, half-starved and deranged. By the turn of the 19th century the estate was heavily in debt, and changed hands a couple of times before the present family inherited it.

The champion Sitka spruce was planted in 1845, and its conical shape and radial branches can be admired in its solitary glory. Other conifers are scattered throughout the woods including another Sitka spruce with huge, head-high surface roots buttressing the trunk, characteristic of native old-growth spruce found in British Columbia. It is there along the Pacific coast that Sitka spruce live up to 600 years and grow up to 90m high. The Tempo tree must not rest on its laurels as there are other trees in Northern Ireland lurking in the wings ready to take its crown.

At 52m high, a Sitka spruce at Tempo Manor is the tallest tree in Northern Ireland

Baunreagh Sitka Spruce Plot

Baunreagh, Slieve Bloom Mountains, Mountrath, County Laois
Picea sitchensis | **Sitka Spruce**

HEIGHT:	45m
GIRTH:	2.3m
ACCESS:	The tree is located on property owned by Coillte and is open for public access in accordance with the company's open-forest policy.

The Slieve Blooms are the only substantial mountains in the centre of Ireland, and the highest point at 527m is Arderin which translates as 'the height of Ireland'. The locals apparently were deluded into thinking that they lived on the slopes of the highest mountain in Ireland. But geological surveys show that the sandstone hills were pushed up to great heights over 300 million years ago and have since worn down which leaves one with the conclusion that midlanders have very long memories.

Today the slopes and valleys are home to the largest continuous conifer plantation in the country, at Baunreagh on the south side in County Laois. Baunreagh gained renown in the 1840s when its land was leased by William Steuart Trench who was one of the most progressive and efficient land agents of his time. He demonstrated how 70 hectares of deep bog could be converted into highly productive arable land with ingenuity and a large workforce. He won awards and acclaim for the largest quantity of wasteland reclaimed in Ireland, and went on to give one of the most vivid eyewitness accounts of the arrival of the potato blight. After the Famine the slopes of Baunreagh reverted to grass, and today some farm buildings, culverts, tracks and lazy beds survive from this remarkable venture.

Later, during the First World War, 750 hectares were purchased at Baunreagh by what was then the Forestry Division of the Department of Lands and planted with conifers. It now contains highly productive timber of Sitka spruce with lodgepole pine on the higher slopes, and ten per cent set aside for biodiversity, along the Delour River. In the centre of the forest is a five-hectare plot containing the most impressive Sitka spruce stand in the country, dating from 1926. The 45m-high trees are preserved for study and as a high-quality seed source for propagation. There is an eeriness standing among these North American giants, as the trunks sway with their tattered tops blotting out the sky. The ground is covered in moss with the occasional fern adding to the feeling of being lost in a land that time has forgotten. A ten-minute walk will take you to the road that links Mountrath with Clonaslee and the contrast is complete.

Worth mentioning is a similar and equally impressive plot of magnificent Sitka spruce trees in Glendine Valley, also located in the Slieve Bloom mountains.

Planted in 1926, a stand of Sitka spruce at Baunreagh in the Slieve Bloom mountains is one of the most impressive in the country

An enormous specimen of golden cypress at Church Cross between Skibbereen and Ballydehob

Golden Cypress at Church Cross

Old Post Office, Church Cross, Skibbereen, County Cork
Cupressus macrocarpa 'Lutea' | **Golden Monterey Cypress**

HEIGHT: 15m
GIRTH: 6.01m
ACCESS: The tree is located on private property but may be viewed from the N71 roadside pull-in at Church Cross between Skibbereen and Ballydehob.

There is a tree erupting out of the garden of the old post office at Church Cross, which lies halfway between Ballydehob and Skibbereen. It is a golden Monterey cypress and instead of doing the decent thing and growing upwards, it has decided to spread over the road in an attempt to hitch a ride back to its home in America. It is the sort of roadside tree to give heart palpitations to passengers on double-decker buses. Monterey cypress, or as some people call them, macrocarpas, have become the largest trees in the Irish landscape since they were introduced nearly two centuries ago.

To call them trees might be an insult to other trees, as so many of them look like shrubs on steroids, and are dark ugly blots on the landscape. They became very popular as hedging and shelter belts around farms and homes, but quickly outgrew their allotted space to become battered arboreal wrecks. With good care and pruning, they can be magnificent domed giants to equal the aristocratic Cedar of Lebanon. Golden varieties like our tree at Church Cross can brighten the gloom of the darkest winter's day and provide shelter and nesting space for any number of birds. Normally they are hardy, but the big freeze in 2010 damaged many inland trees without killing them.

The Monterey cypress was discovered in two small groves on rocky headlands by the Pacific Ocean, south of San Francisco. There they are gnarly and stunted trees, hanging on for dear life against everything the elements throw at them. It is thought that they took a wrong turn from Mexico after the ice sheets melted, and failed to follow the other conifers as they used the Rocky Mountains and coastal ranges to hop, skip and jump to more favourable climate conditions further north. This is one of those species that grows better almost anywhere than its home, and just hung around long enough to be rescued. Now the Church Cross tree is hunkered down as its ancestors have been for thousands of years, and cheering everyone that passes underneath.

Ravensdale Monterey Pine

Ravensdale, Dundalk, County Louth
Pinus radiata | **Monterey Pine**

HEIGHT: 33m

GIRTH: 7.67m

ACCESS: The tree is located on property owned by Coillte and is open for public access in accordance with the company's open-forest policy.

Ravensdale is in the valley of the River Flurry which divides the Cooley Mountains in County Louth from Slieve Gullion in County Armagh. The N1/A1 motorway between Ulster and Leinster or Newry and Dundalk runs through it. The picturesque scenery of wooded slopes and rocky outcrops adds to the dramatic feeling and history about the place. Ravensdale Park was the seat of the Barons Clermont, the biggest landowners in County Louth in the 19th century. In a premonition of dark days to come, the mansion was burnt to the ground during the Civil War in the early 1920s.

Part of the old estate is a forest park open to visitors, and near its entrance a paved cul-de-sac drops down to the river and the West Lodge under the ramparts of the motorway. A few hundred metres to the south is our featured Monterey pine, which is inaccessible to all bar the intrepid. The upper half of the crown stands prominently above surrounding trees and is a landmark for travellers on the motorway. The main trunk is hidden further down the slope, and it is only when one stands at its base that one realises how colossal the tree is. At 7.67m in girth and 33m high it is the largest pine in Ireland with a single stem. Look up and you will see that the craggy ridged trunk divides into huge vertical branches like the pipes of a church organ. The crown is beginning to thin, which suggests that it is past its prime at about 150 years old.

The species of pine was discovered by David Douglas in 1832 at Carmel above Monterey Bay in California. The original trees are now gone, but it was widely planted in Ireland from 1850 onwards, especially in coastal gardens of the south-west. It is the fastest-growing conifer in the world. A tree in New Zealand grew to over 61m in 40 years, while 21m has been recorded in 18 years in Ireland. Unfortunately, pests, disease and late frosts have excluded it from the mix of species suitable for Irish forestry apart from near the coast.

The largest single-stem Monterey pine in Ireland at Ravensdale Forest near Dundalk, County Louth

Sequoia at Powerscourt Waterfall

Powerscourt Waterfall, Enniskerry, County Wicklow
Sequoiadendron giganteum | **Giant Redwood**

HEIGHT: 46m

GIRTH: 7.97m

ACCESS: This tree is located at Powerscourt Waterfall which is open for public access during advertised opening hours. Admission charge.

Before he died in 1904, the seventh Viscount Powerscourt wrote: 'Nobody can say that I have not left my mark on the country.' These words refer to the millions of trees he had planted during his lifetime. He inherited 50,000 acres, and went to work with great energy and imagination in creating one of Ireland's great gardens, and embellishing the Dargle Valley all the way to Powerscourt Waterfall. It was very fortunate that the great age of tree discovery began in the 1830s, so that Viscount Powerscourt had a wonderful new palette to work with.

The greatest tree of them all was found high up in the Sierra Nevada in California in 1852. The sequoia, or giant redwood, can reach 91m high and 30m in girth, and some are 1,500 tonnes in weight. Loggers soon moved in, and cut the most accessible but their massive size helped save them, as the timber shattered when felled. There was little profit and it was possible to preserve them in National Parks and reserves. The coast redwood is a close relative, and an even taller tree of some 115m, which suffered much worse depredations from the lumber industry.

The English called it Wellingtonia, after their military hero and reluctant Irishman, which can't have pleased the Americans or the French. The sequoia is very happy in our climate, and at over a hundred tonnes is already the biggest tree to be found here. The largest in the Dargle Valley is in a line of 23 trees, and is 9m in girth, and was planted in 1861. I have selected the larger of a pair beside the waterfall, for its splendid shape and charming location. It is situated in an open grassy area, which has possibly led to its recent crown dieback due to cars parking underneath it and compacting its roots. A protective fence around should help its survival, and it may become a visitor attraction in its own right.

A giant redwood against the impressive backdrop of Powerscourt Waterfall

Champion Redwood at Woodstock

Woodstock, Inistioge, County Kilkenny
Sequoia sempervirens | **Coast Redwood**

HEIGHT:	42m
GIRTH:	8.2m
ACCESS:	Public during advertised opening hours. For more information visit website: www.woodstock.ie

The sequoia may be the largest tree in the world, but its cousin, the coast redwood, is the tallest at 115m high, which is just shy of the Spire in O'Connell Street, Dublin. There is strong evidence to suggest that the largest coast redwoods were even bigger than the largest sequoias, before being felled in the 19th century in the mad scramble for lumber. The redwood was discovered in 1769 by a Portuguese missionary and there are claims that some trees in Portugal date from then, but seed did not arrive in these islands until 1844, sent by a Russian botanist who had introduced it to the Crimea a few years earlier.

The redwood forest stretches from Big Sur south of San Francisco, all the way north to the Oregon border, a distance of 1,000km, and spreading up to 40km inland. California provides it with ideal growing conditions: summer coastal fogs bathe the tree tops with mist which condenses so that the trees do not have to conduct water from their roots to the towering tops. There is no other forest quite like it, with towering 100m-tall trees standing shoulder to shoulder, blanketing out any ground flora apart from ferns. But so much of the old growth has gone, as its proximity to the coast meant that its high-quality timber was easy to extract.

Soon after their introduction to Ireland, a pair of coast redwoods was planted in Woodstock on a bank above the Monkey Puzzle Avenue. Both are now 8.2m in girth and 42m high, making them the largest in Europe. They obviously enjoy our mild, humid conditions, until they poke their heads above the surrounding shelter, where the exposure stops them in their upward growth. The foliage is like a yew, with regular rows of flat blunt-ended needles, and the redwood is almost unique for a conifer in being able to re-sprout from the stump if cut down. Go and visit these mighty trees in Wood-stock and ponder on these concluding lines from 'The Redwoods' by J. B. Strauss:

An Irish Champion – the coast redwood at Woodstock is the largest of its kind in Europe

> To be like these, straight, true and fine,
> to make our world like theirs, a shrine,
> Sink down, Oh, traveller, on your knees,
> God stands before you in these trees.

Western Red Cedar at Lough Key

Lough Key Forest Park, County Roscommon
Thuja plicata | **Western Red Cedar**

HEIGHT: 31m

GIRTH: 3.44m

ACCESS: The tree is located on property owned by Coillte and is open for public access in accordance with the company's open-forest policy.

Lough Key Forest Park lies beside the southern shore of Lough Key, near the town of Boyle. It was acquired by the state in the 1950s, when it was known as the Rockingham Estate, and had been in the ownership of the Stafford-King-Harmon family for nearly 300 years. Since then the 242-hectare park has been developed as a tourist attraction with a camping and caravan park, with facilities for fishing and boating. In recent years Ireland's only tree-canopy walk has been developed by Coillte and Roscommon County Council, 9m above the ground, which gives you a thrilling bird's-eye perspective on life among trees. There are several rare and champion trees scattered in the parkland, including golden sycamore, variegated horse chestnut and variegated oak. The second largest horse chestnut in the land stands alone in the meadows, while huge old pines, firs, beech and larch are mixed in with the woodland.

The tree that attracts the most attention is a western red cedar beside the path before you reach the woodland trail to Drumman's Island. It is not, in fact, a cedar, but a member of the cypress family from the north Pacific coastline of North America, and was misnamed by lumbermen to add value to its timber. The western red cedar can be easily confused with the Lawson cypress, but differ in their spikier and less dense habit and rosehip-shaped cones.

The Lough Key tree is typical of an open-grown tree, with its tendency to layer its branches, which is best described by Hugh Johnson: 'Their lowest limbs rest on the ground and take root, to spring up and surround the tree with a grove of green buttresses, a tabernacle cavernous and perfumed within, floored and ceilinged in bracken-brown and raftered with branches.'

This tree may well be Ireland's greatest playground. Gently push your children in and you can be safe in the knowledge that you will be forgotten about for as long as you need.

Young visitors to Lough Key Forest Park are drawn to play amongst the layered branches of this western red cedar

Drum Manor Western Hemlock

Drum Manor, Cookstown, County Tyrone
Tsuga heterphylla | **Western Hemlock**

HEIGHT: 37m
GIRTH: 6.15m
ACCESS: Public during advertised opening hours.

Drum Manor Forest Park is on the Drum Road, 4km west of Cookstown. The Forest Service Northern Ireland took over 225 acres (147 hectares) of the landscaped demesne surrounding the early Victorian mansion in the 1960s, and opened it to the public in 1970. They demolished the house in 1975 in order to avoid paying rates, leaving the walls standing, and creating a Japanese garden within. Most of the landscaping and tree planting we see today was carried out in the 1870s by Lord Stuart. One of those trees located a short distance inside the main entrance, forming part of an avenue of conifers, is Ireland's champion western hemlock – by a considerable distance.

Western hemlock is a member of the hemlock family of conifers found in North America and Asia. There are no hemlock trees native to Europe, and we think of hemlock as the toxic weed that poisoned Socrates. They are related to the spruces and it was the eastern hemlock, introduced in 1736 from its home by the Great Lakes, whose fruity aroma resembles the poisonous herb that gives it its name. Hemlock species come in different shapes and sizes, but all have soft delicate foliage and small rounded cones. Western hemlock was seen by plant explorer David Douglas along the Pacific coast in the 1830s, but he took it to be the same species as the eastern hemlock and it was not introduced until 1852. It is the giant of the species at 76m high in the humid rainforests from Oregon to British Columbia, where it is a climax tree in that it can grow in deep shade, waiting for a break in the canopy to shoot up and shade out other species. It does this by having a drooping lead shoot which allows it to grow up unharmed through other trees.

The featured tree at Drum Manor is 37m high and 6.15m in girth, and displays the elegant ranks of soft-sloping branches narrowing to its nodding top which is characteristic of the species. The soft and fine yew-like foliage is brilliant green, and happy in deep shade, making western hemlock one of the most graceful conifers we can grow in Ireland.

Ireland's champion western
hemlock at Drum Manor

Monster Cypress at Ringdufferin

Ringdufferin House, Killyleagh, County Down
Cupressus macrocarpa | **Monterey Cypress**

Height: 31m
Girth: 12.65m
Access: The tree is located on private property. Viewing is by prior appointment only.

Species of the true cypress family are found from Kashmir to the Mediterranean, and Mexico to California in the New World, and have been around for 200 million years. Time, continental drift and climatic change have seen them go their separate ways, and fossil records suggest they all evolved from the Mediterranean cypress. It is hard to believe that the slim, dark columns which dot the classical Mediterranean landscape like exclamation marks could be related to the monster Monterey cypress at Ringdufferin, but then, you could say the same about toy poodles and Great Danes.

Cypresses are very different from other conifers and broadleaf trees in the way they appear to grow so that you cannot see the twigs for the leaves, and they appear to have no buds. The fern-like sprays pause during cold weather, and then set off again in spring to become branches and eventually the branches become trees.

Ringdufferin House sits beside the western shore of Strangford Lough, Ireland's largest sea inlet, which is almost enclosed, but for a narrow channel which allows the tide to race through with such force that it is harnessed to make electricity. The many islands by the western shore are evidence of drowned drumlins, just like the Clew Bay islands in the west of Ireland. Ringdufferin is a beautiful private property, which takes advantage of the mild and relatively dry climate to support a great garden and tree collection. It is here that Ireland's greatest-girthed tree of 12.65m can be found in the shape of a tall broad Monterey cypress planted in the late 19th century. It has a rival of equal girth at Innishannon in County Cork, but that tree slips in my estimation on account of its multi-stem bushiness. That is not to say that the Ringdufferin tree has a perfect single trunk, it is just that this behemoth looks like a tree. Storms have taken huge bites out of the crown, exposing its internal crown structure like a pathologist slicing a brain, and it shows how branches get shaded out and die. You have to admire the growth and vitality of this monster tree that possibly has the greatest volume of timber of any tree in Ireland.

Ireland's greatest-girthed tree – a Monterey cypress at Ringdufferin House with a girth of almost 12.7m

Oregon Maples at Trinity College

College Green, Trinity College Dublin
Acer macrophyllum | **Oregon Maple**

HEIGHT: 16m
GIRTH: 4.11m
ACCESS: This tree is located in the public area of Trinity College Dublin.

The Oregon or bigleaf maple has the largest leaves of any maple, and is also the largest in stature in the world. Some have grown to 49m in the redwood forests of California, while others have girths over 9m in British Columbia. The tree was discovered by Archibald Menzies in 1792, but was not introduced to Europe until the 1830s. Its leaves can be more than a foot across, while the creamy hanging flower clusters burst out in April along with the leaves. Oregon maples grow fast to make respectable trees within 20 years, but like the tulip tree, its branches often split and break during high winds. Coming from a cool humid temperate region, they are particularly happy here in Ireland. The biggest tree known outside its native habitat is found at a private school in County Wicklow. That tree is over 5.1m in girth and 22.9m high with an enormous spread.

At Trinity College several trees were planted about 1850, and were over 40ft (12.2m) high in 1900. Front Square had a matching pair, but one was destroyed during a freak storm in June 1945. It was decided, after a lot of argument, to remove the other for the sake of symmetry. Two Russian rock birch trees were planted as replacements. Go beyond the Campanile to Library Square and admire the magnificent domed Oregon maples in the centre of each lawn. Both are over 4m in girth, and have low spreading branches swelling their trunks. The trees are particularly handsome when they turn a pale yellow in October, and the rustle of their fallen leaves may bring happy memories to many past students.

Oregon Maples in Library Square, Trinity College Dublin

Lough Rynn Tulip Tree

Lough Rynn, County Leitrim
Liriodendron tulipifera | **Tulip Tree**

HEIGHT: 24m

GIRTH: 5.68m

ACCESS: This tree is located on the grounds of Lough Rynn Castle and Estate which is open to the public. For further information see website: www.loughrynn.ie

Lough Rynn Castle and Estate are located on a narrow neck of land between Lough Rynn and Lough Errew, a couple of miles south of the town of Mohill. The property and 92,000 acres (36,421 hectares) spread over four counties were purchased in the 18th century by the Clements family; the house was built in 1833 in the mock-Tudor style. The Clements by this time had risen politically and socially to become the Earls of Leitrim, and in 1839 William Clements took over the management of the estate. In 1854, when his brother died, he became the third Earl, whose name was a byword for authoritarian rule and mistreatment of his tenants, including mass evictions. There were several attempts on his life before he received his comeuppance when he was shot dead in 1878 while visiting his estates in Donegal. The third Earl, despite his faults, obviously loved his trees and many specimens planted at his command, survive today.

The house, gardens and 300 acres (121 hectares) have been developed into a luxury hotel in recent years under new ownership. Hemlocks, holm oaks, cedars and monkey puzzles are scattered throughout the grounds. One of the most impressive trees is an enormous tulip tree, a short distance from the hotel entrance. The tree starts with a squat pale-grey ridged trunk, at 5.7m girth one the largest in the country. Large branches soon erupt out and then twist up to create a broad crown 24m high. The lime-green leaves are extraordinary, as they set off like maple leaves with two side lobes, but where the end lobe should be, it is cut short. The orange-green tulip flowers are usually too high up to be appreciated: the trick is to get a nimble climber to bring some flower sprigs down and float them in a bowl. Tulip trees turn a glorious butter-yellow in autumn, and these qualities make this a beautiful fast-growing tree to plant where space allows.

TREES FROM
THE ORIENT

Traditionally we in Europe have thought of the Orient
as beginning in the Eastern Mediterranean, but as we became
aware of lands beyond, the term shifted east to include Asia,
half of the world's land surface. Many familiar species such as the
black mulberry, common walnut, plane and edible fig originated in
the Near East around the Black Sea and the Caucasus. Unlike North
America, here great mountain ranges run east to west, preventing
numerous tree species from migrating south during the ice age. This
led to mass extinctions, until the mountains flatten out in Burma and
Indo-China. It was here that the great wealth of tree species from
China, Korea and Japan found refuge, and where the greatest array
of temperate trees are found, with new discoveries still being made.
We had to wait until the 18th century before the first Europeans got a
toehold in China and brought back the ginkgo and the first of the
maples, cherries and rhododendrons. China and Japan managed
to keep the West at arm's length for nearly a hundred years,
but eventually the floodgates opened and a great age of
plant discovery began in the late 19th century.

Ginkgo at Anna Livia Mills

Annalivia Mills, Lucan, County Dublin
Ginkgo biloba | **Maidenhair Tree**

HEIGHT: 22m
GIRTH: 4.16m
ACCESS: The tree is located on property in the ownership of Fingal County Council but is not currently open for public access. Viewing can be arranged by prior appointment only.

Dublin's green artery runs along the River Liffey from Islandbridge through Chapelizod to Lucan. It is nature's thoroughfare from the country into the big smoke. A mile before Lucan is the former Anna Livia Flour Mills which was operated by the Shackleton family, cousins of the famous Antarctic explorer Ernest Shackleton. The mill is now owned by Fingal County Council who hope to restore and open it as an industrial heritage site sometime in the future. In front of the miller's house stands Ireland's greatest ginkgo.

The ginkgo or maidenhair tree is a single species of a single order, which predates the other two orders of conifers and broadleaf trees. It has been around for over 250 million years, and you have to admire its tenacity in surviving continental drift, dinosaurs, meteor strikes and several ice ages. It has outlived its enemies, pests and disease, and its viability must be due to its perfect design. It once was widespread throughout the northern hemisphere but had retreated to remote mountains in China by the time humans appeared. Luckily for us, the Chinese appreciated its uniqueness enough to plant it as a sacred tree beside their temples. It was introduced to the west in 1730, and the oldest trees in Ireland date from the mid-19th century. It needs hot summers to thrive, so in Ireland nearly all our best trees are found in walled gardens which retain the heat.

The Anna Livia ginkgo was planted about 1880 and is 22m high and over 4m in girth. Its half-moon-shaped leaves turn a gorgeous yellow before falling in November. Even more remarkable is its curious trunk, which appears to be melting like an old wax candle. The Chinese call these *chi-chi*: lumps and nodules which are characteristic of ancient trees. They do not seem to serve any purpose and are just another element which makes ginkgo the unique tree it is.

A Ginkgo tree at the Anna Livia Mills near Lucan, County Dublin

Caucasian Elm at Glasnevin

National Botanic Gardens, Glasnevin, Dublin
Zelkova serrata | **Caucasian Elm**

HEIGHT: 20m
GIRTH: 4.27m
ACCESS: Public during advertised opening hours.

The iconic or signature tree in the National Botanic Gardens has to be the zelkova or Caucasian elm in front of the herbarium / library building. The zelkova family of trees are related to the elms, but have proved more resistant to Dutch elm disease. The Caucasian elm is native to the mountain slopes of southern Russia and northern Iran. During the Ice Age this region became a refuge for many species of trees found nowhere else. The rest of Eurasia had mountain ranges running east to west, which prevented many species now extinct from retreating from the ice.

All Caucasian elms in Ireland have one inexplicable feature: they are shaped like an upturned paint brush. They have a deeply fluted short trunk from which hundreds of vertical stems erupt and then spray out like a fountain near the top. No trees of this shape have been found in its native woods, where they all have conventional single trunks. Perhaps when it was introduced in 1760 all the seed was collected from a single eccentric tree or maybe it is a response to a change in environment.

The tree in Glasnevin is the Irish champion at 4.3m girth and 20m high. It was 9 feet (2.7m) in girth in 1905, which suggests that it must be nearly 200 years of age, one of the garden's oldest trees. Only three other mature trees are known in Ireland: a second tree in Glasnevin, another in Rostrevor, County Down and a mystery tree in the Glen of Aherlow in County Tipperary. I found it by chance at an obscure T-junction, and local research found that this site was once an entrance to a British military barracks. Perhaps it was brought back from a foreign posting and was planted to commemorate a person or event. These days many young trees are being planted in collections and I can't think of a more bizarre-shaped tree to grab people's attention.

The extraordinary fluted trunk of the Caucasian Elm in the National Botanic Gardens, Glasnevin

Cashel Palace Mulberry

Cashel Palace Hotel, Cashel, County Tipperary
Morus nigra | **Black Mulberry**

HEIGHT: 8m

GIRTH: 1.78m

ACCESS: The tree is located on private property but may be accessed by guests and patrons of Cashel Palace Hotel.

The black or common mulberry has been in cultivation for its luscious, richly flavoured fruit for thousands of years. It probably originated in the Black Sea region, and is now found all over the temperate world. Introduced here in the 17th century, the two trees at Cashel Palace Hotel are the oldest known with a planting date. Planted in 1702 to commemorate the coronation of Queen Anne, they may be seen on the front lawn of the Bishop's Palace, facing the Rock of Cashel. Archbishop Bolton was eventually able to view the trees from his newly built palace in the 1730s. The palace has been a luxury hotel since 1962, and many celebrities have been photographed admiring the trees. But what they admire now bears no relation to what the original trees looked like.

Mulberry trees have a reputation for growing very slowly to a great age but in reality they grow fast and their trunks decay before they reach 100 years. This phenomenon is explained by the traditional method of propagation of pushing a large cut branch into the ground: sprouts quickly emerge to make a fruiting low tree. Eventually its branches layer and take root to form a ring of trees, while the mother tree decays. The gnarly branches and handsome leaves that turn yellow in autumn add up to a tree that looks ancient and full of character.

The other mulberry in cultivation is from China, and is called the white mulberry, *Morus alba*. It is potentially a much bigger tree but its growth is limited by our cool summers. This is the tree that silkworms are fed on. The worms or caterpillars produce a very fine thread to make their cocoon which is then collected and spun to make silk. At Mount St Joseph's Abbey near Roscrea white mulberry trees survive today from experimental silk production in the 1940s. The monks produced enough silk to make some clerical vestments.

A mulberry tree at Cashel Place Hotel, planted in 1702

Magnolia at Lismore

Lismore Castle, Lismore, County Waterford
Magnolia campbellii | **Campbell's magnolia**

ACCESS: This tree is located on private property, the grounds of which are open for public access during advertised opening hours. Lismore Castle itself remains a private home and is not open to visitors. For more information visit website: www.lismorecastlegardens.com

The beautiful town of Lismore is best approached from the bridge over the Blackwater. A short distance west of the bridge, pull in and enjoy a wonderful view of the romantic battlements of Lismore Castle which seem to float above the river. In the foreground various trees are scattered in the meadows, one of which takes on a whole new persona in March. It is then that this bare tree has a flock of flamingos roosting on every twig and branch. Rub your eyes and it is soon apparent that this magnificent spectacle is an early flowering *Magnolia campbellii,* with pink flowers the size of dinner plates. This aristocrat among magnolias comes from the Himalaya where it towers over the rhododendron forest in clouds of white or pink flowers.

Introduced to the west about 1870, it first flowered in Europe at the lost gardens at Lakelands near Cork city before the turn of the century. It is perfectly hardy anywhere in Ireland, but it needs frost-free conditions when flowering, or else the blossoms turn to mush, which can be guaranteed only in coastal gardens. This particular tree is quite young and of moderate size. Some have already reached 24m but they all take about 30 years before first flowering.

Other trees to look for in the meadows are silver maples, swamp cypresses and champion dawn redwood and red maple. Up at the castle you can visit the walled gardens where even larger magnolias are found. There is a notable yew walk, over 300 years old, and a working kitchen garden in continuous use for 400 years.

I have a ten-year-old Campbell's magnolia collected from seed from this tree. The secret to its eventual flowering is planting it in a cold shady spot where the buds will not be wooed open by the spring sunshine too soon.

The magnificent flowers of *Magnolia campbellii*
at Lismore Castle, County Waterford

Cryptomeria at Fota

Fota House, Arboretum & Gardens, Fota Island, Carrigtwohill, County Cork
Cryptomeria japonica 'Spiralis' | **Japanese Red Cedar**

HEIGHT: 20m
GIRTH: 2.51m
ACCESS: Public during advertised opening hours.

Fota gets its name from the Irish *'fod te'*, which translates as 'warm soil'. It is this great advantage, combined with the mild climate, which attracted the Smith-Barry family to turn their hunting lodge into a Regency mansion in the 1820s and create the ornamental gardens and arboretum. Fota is an island in Cork Harbour linked by a causeway to Great Island and Cobh. The arboretum, as the name might suggest, is not an arranged collection but a parkland planted with incredible tree specimens from around the world with space to be admired from all directions. From the 1850s Lord Barrymore specialised in newly introduced frost-sensitive trees, and his work was continued by Mrs Dorothy Bell up to the 1970s. After her death University College Cork looked after the arboretum, while its future hung in the balance. It is now being revitalised by the Office of Public Works, and open to the public as one of Ireland's great tree collections, renowned by tree lovers the world over. It has so many Irish and even European champions, including *Magnolia campbelli, Dacrydium, Cinnamomum, Torreya* and pine species that to choose one over the rest seems unfair. But every time I see the *Cryptomeria japonica* 'Spiralis' it takes my breath away. Its dense blobs of foliage rise up 20m, like a billowing thundercloud, apparently without the frame one normally associates with a conifer tree. This cultivar was introduced in 1860 from Japan, and usually forms a slow-growing bush of dense habit. It is also called 'Granny's ringlets' because the leaves are spirally twisted around the stem.

Cryptomeria or Japanese red cedar is not a true cedar but a distant relative of the redwood family. It drifted north from the old continent Gondwanaland on its break-up, and is the Japanese equivalent of the sequoia, with its great age and size making it Asia's largest tree. It has been recorded over 76m high and 21m in girth. It is the mainstay of Japan's timber forests, which have been managed for hundreds of years. *Cryptomerias* are also called *'sugi'* ('cedars') in Japan where huge old specimens are revered, and planted by shrines. They prefer rainfall all year round, which is why all the best specimens are found in the Azores, and the south-west of Ireland. Two trees in Curraghmore, County Waterford and Caher House in County Clare at 6m girth compete to be the largest in Ireland. At the other extreme, a low bushy 'Elegans' cultivar covers over 0.2 hectares at Kilmacurragh in County Wicklow.

A rare specimen of the spiral-leaved Japanese red cedar, *Cryptomeria japonica* 'Spiralis', at Fota Arboretum in Cork

Dawn Redwood at Glasnevin

National Botanic Gardens, Glasnevin, Dublin
Metasequoia glyptostroboides | **Dawn Redwood**

HEIGHT: 16m
GIRTH: 2.23m
ACCESS: Public during advertised opening hours.

In 1941, a Japanese botanist described *Metasequoia* as a fossil from the Mesozoic era, and separated it from redwoods and swamp cypress. Little did he know that at the same time a Chinese forester surveying in Szechuan province had come across a strange deciduous conifer. The tree was bare and he asked the local schoolmaster to send samples in the post next year. These were lost but further samples were collected in 1944, but because of the war were not studied till 1946, when it was confirmed as a new species. It was a botanical sensation, to find that this extinct fossil still existed, and was heralded as a 'living fossil'. Imagine a zookeeper waking up one morning to find a dinosaur munching on his elephants! That might be an extreme analogy but botanists can get really excited about such occurrences. In the autumn of 1947 the Arnold arboretum in Boston funded an expedition to collect seed, which was distributed around the world in 1948 to other botanical institutions. It was not a moment too soon, as China closed its borders to foreigners after the revolution in 1949.

Metasequoia was given the English name of 'dawn redwood', indicating its family ties to the redwoods of America. By 1950 several trees were planted in Ireland, including Birr Castle, County Offaly, Brook Hall in Derry, Glasnevin in Dublin and the Japanese Gardens in Kildare. The Glasnevin tree has the classic cone shape and fluted trunk, while in autumn it turns a foxy red-brown colour. You can see it beside the pond, which should be an ideal location but at 2.2m girth and 16m high it is one of the smaller of the early trees. Bigger trees of over 3m girth are found in Counties Antrim, Cork, Meath and Waterford, while the tallest at 26m is in Powerscourt, County Wicklow. So far they are growing as fast as their redwood cousins, and could potentially grow to 45m. Like the ginkgo they have conquered their enemies of pests and disease, and will become huge old trees for our descendants to enjoy.

Close-up of the leaves of dawn redwood

One of the earliest introductions to Ireland of dawn redwood planted in 1948 at the National Botanic Gardens, Glasnevin

Adare Manor Cedar

Adare Manor Hotel & Golf Club, Adare, County Limerick
Cedrus libanii | **Cedar of Lebanon**

HEIGHT: 19m
GIRTH: 10.25m
ACCESS: The tree is located on private property but may be accessed by guests and patrons of Adare Manor Hotel.

The Cedar of Lebanon is the fabled tree in the Bible, used to build palaces and other important buildings. King Solomon built the great Temple of Jerusalem entirely of cedar. It was ruthlessly exploited, so that only a few small groves still existed on Mount Lebanon by the 17th century. More extensive forests in south-east Turkey escaped the attention of the timber merchants due to their isolation but they all suffered from goat grazing.

The cedar was introduced into Britain in the mid-17th century, and the earliest planted is a matter of debate, claim and counterclaim. This is a tree species that inspires poetry, is lauded for its quality timber, and sought after to adorn the lawn of every country pile. Even the cedar featured here at Adare gets in on the act, with the great tree expert Alan Mitchell writing that it was thought to have been planted in 1645, but that nothing was known of its history. The fact that it is 10.2m in girth, and the Irish champion, might give that claim some credibility but closer inspection suggests that its girth measurement is exaggerated because of several stems forking almost to the ground.

I counted 180 rings on a very large branch recently removed from 2.1m above the ground. Add another ten years for the young tree to get to that height and 1820 is the possible planting date. This should not lessen the tree's merit, as it is a magnificent tree overhanging the River Maigue, and beautifully complements the Adare Manor Hotel. It has an elegant symmetrical crown, with wide horizontal branches sweeping its own reflection in the river.

The house, now a hotel, is a Tudor-Revival manor, built for the Earls of Dunraven between 1832 and 1862 to replace an early 17th-century house. The grounds have other notable trees, such as cork oak, Monterey cypress, liquidambar, weeping beech, yew and the only espaliered ginkgo in the country.

Cedar is so highly prized around the world that timber merchants have given totally unrelated trees the name cedar. There are only four true cedar species, and two of them, the Atlas from North Africa and the Cypriot, have been reduced to geographical subspecies of Cedar of Lebanon by many botanists. Identifying them by their first letter and shape helps distinguish them so that A in Atlas stands for ascending branches, L in Lebanon for level branches and D in Deodar for drooping branches, but the method is not foolproof.

The Cedar of Lebanon alongside the River Maigue at Adare Manor

References

Bean, W. J., 1970, 1973 and 1976. *Trees & Shrubs Hardy In The British Isles* Volumes 1, 2 and 3, 8th edition. John Murray, London.

Bence-Jones, Mark, 1988. *A Guide To Irish Country Houses* revised edition. Constable, London.

Browne, Dinah, 1999. *Our Remarkable Trees*. Trees of Time and Place, Belfast.

Cabot, David, 1999. *Ireland*. HarperCollins, London.

Carey, Michael, 2009. *If Trees Could Talk*. Coford, Dublin.

Carmichael, Rosie, 1995. Avenues from the Past to the Future. *Arboricultural Journal* Vol. 19, pp. 111–120.

Couch, Sarah M., 1992. The Practice of Avenue Planting in the Seventeenth and Eighteenth Centuries. *Garden History* Vol. 20 (2), pp. 173–200.

Elwes, Henry John & Henry, Augustine, 2012. *The Trees Of Great Britain And Ireland*. The Society of Irish Foresters, County Wicklow. Facsimile Edition.

Feehan, John, 1979. *The Landscape of Slieve Bloom*. Blackwater Press, Dublin.

Forbes, A. C., 1933. *Tree Planting In Ireland During Four Centuries*. Proceedings of the Royal Irish Academy. Vol. 41 C6 168–199.

Fitzpatrick, H. M., 1933. *The Trees Of Ireland – Native And Introduced*. Scientific Proceedings of the Royal Dublin Society Vol. 20 [41] 597–656.

Hageneder, Fred, 2007. *Yew: A History*. Sutton Publishing, Gloucestershire.

Hayes, Samuel, 2003. *Practical Treatise on Trees*. New Island, Dublin. Facsimile Edition.

Hight, Julian, 2011. *Britain's Tree Story*. National Trust, London.

Hyams, Edward, 1967. *Irish Gardens*. Macdonald, London.

Johnson, Hugh, 1973. *The International Book of Trees*. Mitchell Beazley, London.

Johnson, Owen, 2011. *Champion Trees of Britain & Ireland*. Kew Publishing, Kew.

Liddy, Pat. 1998. *Walking Dublin*. New Holland Publishers, London.

Loudon, J. C., 1844. *Arboretum et Fruticetum Britannicum*. J. C. Louden, London.

Mabey, Richard, 2007. *Beechcombings*. Vintage, London.

McCullen, John A., 2009. *An Illustrated History of The Phoenix Park Landscape and Management to 1880*. Office of Public Works, Government Publications, Ireland.

Magner, Donal, 2011. *Stopping By Woods*. The Lilliput Press, Dublin.

Malins, Edward and The Knight of Glin, 1976. *Lost Demesnes Irish Landscape Gardening 1660–1845*. Barrie & Jenkins Ltd, London.

Malins, Edward and Patrick Bowe, 1980. *Irish Gardens and Demesnes from 1830*. Barrie & Jenkins, London.

Miles, Archie, 1999. *Silva: The Tree in Britain*. Ebury Press, London.

Mitchell, Alan, 1996. *Trees of Britain*. Harper Collins Publishers, London.

Morton, Andrew, 1998. *Tree Heritage of Britain And Ireland*. Swan Hill Press, Shrewsbury.

Nelson, E. Charles, 1993. *Trees of Ireland: Native and Naturalized*. The Lilliput Press, Dublin.

Nelson, E. Charles, 2009. *An Irishman's Cuttings*. The Collins Press, Cork.

Pakenham, Thomas, 1996 and 2002. *Meeting With Remarkable Trees*. George Weidenfeld & Nicholson Ltd, London.

Pim, Sheila, 1966. *The Wood and The Trees*. Macdonald, London.

Phibbs, John, 1991. 'Groves and Belts', *Garden History* Vol. 19 (2) pp. 175–186.

Reeves-Smith, Terence, 2001. *Gardens of Ireland*. Mitchell Beazley, London.

Simon, Ben, 2009. *If Trees Could Talk*. The Forest of Belfast, Belfast.

Simon, Ben, 2013. *Tales, Traditions and Folklore of Ireland's Trees*. The Forest of Belfast, Belfast.

Thomas, Graham Stuart, 1979. 'Avenues and Trees', *Gardens of the National Trust*. Book Club Associates, London.

Tree Register of Ireland, 2005. *Champion Trees*. Tree Council of Ireland, Dublin.

Tudge, Colin, 2005. *The Secret Life of Trees*. Penguin Allen Lane, London.

Van Pelt, Robert, 2001. *Forest Giants of The Pacific Coast*. Global Forest, Washington.

Zucchelli, Christine, 2009. *Trees of Inspiration*. The Collins Press, Cork.

Website

www.aviewoncities.com/berlin/unterdenlinden.htm, accessed on 3 June 2013.

Acknowledgements

The genesis for this book was the survey of Heritage Trees in Ireland initiated in 2009 by the Tree Register of Ireland and carried out by Aubrey Fennell with early assistance from Kate Crane. The project is led by the Tree Council of Ireland, in association with the Irish Tree Society and was initially part-funded by the Heritage Council and Crann.

This book is a cooperative venture spearheaded by the Tree Register of Ireland monitoring committee which includes John McLoughlin (Chairman), Aubrey Fennell, Dr Mary Forrest, Dr Matthew Jebb, Dr Christy Boylan, Liam P. O'Flanagan, Philip Harvey, Patricia Flanagan and Mary Keenan, all of whom have kindly contributed their time and expertise to the book in various ways.

The author and the Tree Council of Ireland are hugely indebted and grateful to the board and management of the Kerry Group for their generous sponsorship, without which this book would not have reached its fruition. We would also like to thank the Society of Irish Foresters and the Irish Tree Society for their early financial support of the venture.

We want especially to thank all the owners and custodians of the various trees for their willing assistance in providing access and information to us. They are the caretakers of this unique heritage. Thanks to Geoff Power who undertook early research for the project and to George Cunningham, Mary Davies, Carmel Duignan, Alistair Pfeifer and Donal Magner for reviewing early versions of scripts. We particularly thank Alannah Hopkin for her help and thorough attention to detail in editing and correcting the draft text.

Our thanks to Thomas Pakenham for writing the foreword and to Dr Christy Boylan for his input of information and text for the chapter on 'Great Avenues & Historic Landscapes'. We are also grateful to Cormac Foley, Niall Foley, David Alderman and Templeport Development Association for their permission to use photographs which they have contributed to the book.

We would like to acknowledge the members of the Tree Council of Ireland, especially Eanna Ní Lamhna (President), Terry O'Connor and Michael O'Brien for their unstinting support and interest in the project and we thank the publishers The Collins Press.

Our book *Heritage Trees of Ireland* is the result of the work of a very dedicated team. Aubrey Fennell wrote the text. Like a human dynamo he traverses the landscape seeking hidden trees that have a story to tell and exudes a clear passion and deep familiarity with trees. Carsten Krieger and Kevin Hutchinson travelled the country and endured the unpredictability of our Irish weather to take their wonderful photographs which enhance the stories. Patricia Flanagan provided much valued administrative support and Mary Keenan managed the production of the project, driving it along gently, arranging funding, compiling and editing the scripts, collating the images and much more besides.

In conclusion, to all those above who have contributed to the project and to anybody whom we very regrettably may have omitted to mention, we reiterate our thanks.

The Tree Council
of Ireland

Tree Council
of Ireland

Photograph credits

Carsten Krieger: pp. 2, 19, 23, 25, 26, 29, 33, 34, 36, 39, 41, 43, 44, 47, 55, 59, 60, 62, 65, 66, 73, 77, 78, 79, 83, 87, 88, 91, 93, 94, 98, 101, 102, 110, 113, 114, 117, 121, 122, 129, 133, 134, 137, 149, 150, 153, 154, 157, 163, 167, 168, 171, 172, 175, 186 (both), 190, 193, 204, 212 (both), 215, 223, 224, 234, 236, 237, 242, 250, 255, 260, 263, 266 (all), 269, 270, 273, 278, 281, 287, 288, 292, 294, 295, 300, 303, 304, 309, 316 and 325.

Kevin J. Hutchinson: pp. 20, 30, 48 (both), 51, 56, 69, 70, 74 (both), 84, 97, 104, 105, 106, 107, 124, 125, 126 (both), 130, 131, 138, 141, 142, 145, 146, 158 (both), 164, 176, 180, 181, 182, 185, 189, 194, 197, 200, 203 (both), 207, 208, 211, 216, 219, 220, 221, 227, 228, 233, 238, 245, 249, 251, 253, 259, 274, 276, 277, 284, 290, 291, 297, 298, 299, 307, 312, 313, 314, 315, 319 (both), 321 (both), 322 and 323.

Cormac Foley: p. 108.

David Alderman p. 109.

Niall Foley: p. 241.

Templeport Development Association: p. 256 (both).